SOUL ENERGY

Awakening the Light Within Your 5th Dimensional Guide

Cara Elliott HealingHouse

2024 - 2026 Edition

CARAELLIOTTHEALINGHOUSE.COM

Please note this is for personal use only.
Any use of information in this book is at the reader's discretion and risk. The author or publisher take no legal responsibility for the effectiveness results or benefits of the content of this book, nor do they make any promises, warranties or guarantees about the results of suggestions made.
A reminder that all energy healing and information offered in this publication is not a substitute for appropriate medical or psychological care. Always seek medical / psychological advice when and where appropriate.

The Author acknowledges the illustrations used from Designrr and Dreamstime.

Copyright ©2024 by Cara Elliott Healing House

No part of this publication may be reproduced, distributed, or transmitted in any form or by any means, including photocopying, recording or other electronic or mechanical methods, without the prior written permission of the author.

ISBN: 978-0-473-70778-1

Printed in Australia by IngramSpark
1st Edition

CARAELLIOTTHEALINGHOUSE.COM

About the Author

CARA ELLIOTT is a Soul-Life Coach, Spiritual teacher, Training Facilitator, PSYCH-K® and ThetaHealing™ Practitioner, Energy Healer, Author and Speaker.
With over 25 years of experience helping people globally, to bring harmony and wellbeing to their mental, emotional, physical and energetic 'bodies'.

Through her Wellness Retreats and Spiritual Development Workshops, Cara empowers people to believe in themselves and their ability to create a life aligned with their dreams and soul's purpose. Cara has developed a deep understanding of the interconnectedness between the universal Source and the spiritual energies that influence our lives.

As a pioneer in Soul - Life Coaching and Quantum LightWorker, Cara has supported thousands of people to 'awaken' and raise their vibration through individual and group healing sessions.
Cara has also featured on iHeart Radio discussing all things Energy and the shift into the 5th dimension.

The energy flowing into the planet in the past 12 years is of a much higher frequency than before and Cara continues to upgrade her own energy bodies to be able to receive and channel this energy in her healing practices.

CARAELLIOTTHEALINGHOUSE.COM

A Note to the Reader

Dear Reader,
This Book is a practical guide to Transformation - a shift from the 3rd to the 5th dimension 2024 - 2026.

As a Soul | Life Coach and Energy Healer for over 25yrs, I have witnessed many beautiful souls transform their lives to align with their heart's desires. and raise their vibrations. It is to these courageous people that I dedicate this book.

This book is a guide to assist you in this transformation. I have been asked by my spiritual and galactic guides, to 'show the way' and share my wisdom and experience as a Light worker, of how we can Raise our Vibration to live in the 5th Dimensional Frequencies.

In navigating the ascension process, this book offers guidelines to step into your Light worker role, to integrate and expand your awareness, and to embrace the 5th Dimensional frequencies in your day-to-day life.
This book offers explanations of what the 5th dimension is, what you can do to raise your vibration with free meditations and pdf guides to assist you on this journey.

My wish is that this book opens up new perspectives and a new way of living – a portal to the 5th Dimension.

In Love and Light *Cara*

Table of Contents

Chapter 1:
Multidimensional Transformation — 7

Chapter 2:
Awakening to Your True Self — 17

Chapter 3:
Navigating the Ascension Process — 25

Chapter 4: Resources and Practices
for 5th Dimensional Expansion — 37

Chapter 5:
Stepping into Your Lightworker Role — 55

Chapter 6: Integration and Expansion — 65

Chapter 7:
Embracing the 5th Dimension — 73

References & Resources — 83

Chapter 1: Multidimensional Transformation
- Unveiling the Mysteries of Higher Consciousness
- The Shift from 3rd to 5th Dimension
- Characteristics of the 5th Dimension
- The Importance of 5th Dimensional Expansion

Chapter 2: Awakening to Your True Self
- Embracing Your Authenticity
- Letting Go of Limiting Beliefs
- Connecting with Your Higher Self
- Cultivating Self-Acceptance and Self-Love

Chapter 3: Navigating the Ascension Process
- Recognizing Ascension Symptoms
- Balancing Your Energy Centres
- Embracing the Power of Forgiveness

Chapter 4: Resources & Practices for 5th Dimensional Expansion
- Cultivating Inner Peace and Connection
- Meditation
- Mindfulness
- Energy Healing Techniques
- Surrounding Yourself with Positivity
- Connecting with Nature and the Elements
- Using high vibrational Crystals

Chapter 5: Stepping into Your Lightworker Role
- Recognizing the Interconnectedness of All Beings
- Understanding Your Soul's Purpose
- Sharing Your Gifts and Talents
- Serving Others with Compassion
- Practicing Compassion / Empathy
- Being a Beacon of Light and Hope

Chapter 6: Integration and Expansion
- Embracing the Integration Process
- Embodying Higher Frequencies
- Manifesting Abundance in All Areas of Life
- Trusting the Divine Timing of Your Soul's Journey

Chapter 7: Embracing the 5th Dimension
- Navigating the Shift in Consciousness
- Anchoring Light and Love on Earth
- Radiating Positivity and Peace
- Co-creating a New Earth in the 5th Dimension

References & Resources

Chapter 1: Multidimensional Transformation

Unveiling the Mysteries of Higher Consciousness

Welcome, light workers, healers, way-showers, and awakening souls, to the fascinating world of "Awakening the Light Within: Your 5th Dimensional Guide." In this transformational book, we delve into the depths of the 5th dimension, unlocking its mysteries and offering insights to support YOUR journey as you expand and raise your vibration into the 5th dimensional frequency.

We find ourselves in a pivotal space between 2024 - 2026 where we are balancing between the remnants of the past and the threshold of a new Golden Age of New Earth. Unlike any time before, the year 2024 offers us a profound opportunity to prepare our hearts and minds for the new reality unfolding around us. Raising our vibrations to live in the 5th dimensional reality. I am told (by my guides) that 2024 is a year of immense potentiality waiting to be materialized as all- possibilities, embedded with the invigorating and jubilant energy of '8' (numerologically speaking).

We are in the ascension age now and no longer waiting to awaken and raise our vibrations. Some of you have been on the path for a long time, others are new and wondering if this is all 'crazy and weird' nonsense but can' keep away from it as your soul pulls you back. It is not new – we have all been on this path many, many lifetimes. There is no one more important than another, we are all divine, important, and needed, each in our own way.

As we expand into the 5th dimension, a realm of higher consciousness, a vibrational frequency that transcends the limitations of our physical reality, we will find our way. It is a state of being where love, unity, and interconnectedness prevail, and the veil between the spiritual and physical worlds becomes increasingly thin. As you embark on your journey of 5th dimensional expansion, it is crucial to understand its essence and how it can shape your perception of reality.

CARAELLIOTTHEALINGHOUSE.COM

Within the 5th dimension, time and space are more fluid, and the boundaries of the ego dissolve, allowing for a deeper connection with your authentic self. Here, you tap into your divine potential, awakening dormant gifts and abilities that have resided within you since time immemorial. It is a realm where intuition reigns supreme, and synchronicities become the language of the universe, guiding you towards your highest path.

To explore the 5th dimension, it is vital to cultivate a conscious awareness of your thoughts, emotions, and energy. The power of intention and manifestation amplifies exponentially, enabling you to co-create your reality with the universe. As you align your vibrations with the frequencies of love, compassion, and gratitude, you radiate light and attract experiences that mirror your elevated state of being.

During this exciting era the collective consciousness is undergoing a profound shift towards the 5th dimension. The veils of illusion are lifting, revealing a world guided by unity, peace, and harmony. As light workers, healers, and way-showers, your role becomes increasingly significant. Your awakening souls hold the keys to unlocking the collective potential for transformation, serving as beacons of light in a world ready for spiritual growth.

Together we will look at into various techniques, and practices to support your 5th dimensional expansion. From meditation and energy healing to conscious manifestation and soul connection, we will provide you with practical guidance and resources to navigate this extraordinary journey. Through personal anecdotes as a Soul Coach, ancient wisdom, and cutting-edge research, we aim to empower and inspire you as you embark on this transformational path.

Prepare to unlock the limitless potential within you as we embark on this exploration of the 5th dimension. Together, we will illuminate the path towards awakening the light within and manifesting a reality aligned with Love, Grace, and infinite possibilities. The time has come to embrace your Soul's purpose and lead the way towards a world where the 5th Dimension is a living reality for all.

In the first half of 2024 we will experience more dimensional gateways converging and thus, timelines merging, giving rise to a valuable opportunity to expand our consciousness and energetic bodies exponentially. A whole spectrum of frequencies – from galaxies and stars to deities and elements – can prevail to activate the remembrance and revival of a galactic-human race on earth.

The Shift from 3rd to 5th Dimension

In the realm of spiritual growth and enlightenment, the concept of dimensions holds immense significance. As light workers, healers, way-showers, and awakening souls, we are constantly seeking to expand our consciousness and tap into higher realms of existence. The shift from the 3rd to the 5th dimension is a profound transformation that holds immense potential for our personal and collective evolution.

The 3rd dimension, characterized by duality, separation, and ego-driven consciousness, has been the predominant reality on Earth for centuries. The physical self and spiritual self are intertwined and cannot be separated, only the illusion of separation can stand in the 3rd dimension. Now is the time for the illusion to stand no more. As truth is being revealed to those with eyes to see, ears to hear and action to take. A collective action to rise and ascend into the 5th dimension.

When we 'awaken' we step out of identification with our thinking mind and become present. It is a shift in consciousness where thinking and awareness become separate. Meditation is one many powerful practice we can use for 'awakening', as it allows us to question the assumptions of the mind.

As we enter the year 2024, a powerful cosmic alignment is paving the way for a monumental shift into the 5th dimension. Physical existence is based upon cycles. The same way it takes us 26,000 (Mayan Calendar) years to complete an evolutionary cycle, the global pandemics, conflicts, racial intolerance and other planetary events we are currently facing also happen in cycles. Some say we are in the closing stages of Kali Yug, also referred to as the age of darkness and chaos.

This shift marks a transition from fear-based living to love-based living, from limitation to boundless potential, and from illusion to divine truth. You can make these transformations in current spiritual space, without physically relocating. You can improve not only your health but enrich your career and love life, turning your environment into a powerhouse of success. The 5th dimension awaits your presence, your love, and your light. Open your hearts, expand your consciousness, and step into the limitless realm of possibilities that awaits you in 2024 and beyond.

In the 5th dimension, unity consciousness prevails. We recognize the interconnectedness of all beings and the inherent divinity within each soul. Love and Acceptance become the guiding force in our lives, and we cultivate compassion, empathy, and forgiveness towards ourselves and others. We become conscious co-creators, harnessing the power of our thoughts and intentions to manifest our highest visions and dreams.

There is a window of opportunity in 2024 where we need to be in our 'lane', in alignment with our truth. The crisscross and interface of our realities on the planet has created a feeling of instability, a wobble if you like. The purpose of the wobble of time is to condense and bring together, information that is needed to truly propel and transcend us forward.

When this influx of plasma energy comes into this planet and our cells are flooded with this light, we can receive it and integrate this energy information into your physical and light bodies more quickly and with ease and Grace.

This energy information will be available to all of us, when we are aware and 'holding the space' for expansion with our intention and practices, we will move through this growth stage more easily. We don't need to 'fall apart' during this ascension / expansion process.

- Nothing can be retained in our bodies that is not in alignment with your higher-self and your highest potential.

- Lots of people will be spontaneously ready to receive channeled information. Be open to receive this information as you align with your soul's plan and purpose.

- Use nature to help support and ground you. There is lots of information in mother earth, so open to receive from the earth through grounding with your Earth Star Chakra.

As we embark on this journey of 5th dimension expansion, it is essential to release old patterns, beliefs, and attachments that no longer serve our growth and expansion. We must heal our emotional wounds, transcend our fears, and embrace the light within us. This process requires inner work, self-reflection, and a commitment to personal transformation.

> *'Self' is the only human aspect you can truly change. Change, at this point in human evolution is absolute.*

Within the individual-self is where the most profound transformation occurs. When we move past trauma issues, memory, buried emotions from the present and past incarnations and future trajectories, we move into the 5th Dimensional energies of peace. Here lies the introspective energies of true transformation.

In the 5th dimension, time is experienced differently. We move beyond linear time and enter the realm of the eternal present moment. Past traumas and future anxieties lose their grip on us as we fully immerse ourselves in the beauty and perfection of the present moment. This shift allows us to access higher realms of consciousness, tap into our intuitive abilities, and receive guidance from our higher selves and our spiritual guides.

The transition to the 5th dimension is not without its challenges. It requires courage, perseverance, and a deep trust in your Soul's divine plan. However, the rewards are immeasurable. As we awaken to our true nature as divine beings of light, we become beacons of love and transformation, inspiring others to embark on their own journey of awakening. Sharing information and living the example, gives people choices. They can choose to apply this information in their lives to experience the expansion or choose to ignore it. It is their soul's choice on their soul's journey.

The majority of humanity are awakening and are excited to ascend and raise their vibration to a place where joy and peace exists. We are in the new way of being, and light workers, energy healers and awakened souls are helping those who are still coming to this space of 'change'. Talk and connect with others and share your wisdom and experiences.

A galactic event this year will be so profound, it will radiate out and infuse light to other planets around us. It ripples out into the cosmos, to our universe and to all the galaxies. At the same time connect to those sentient beings on our planet. Nature, animals crystals etc..

Hermetic Philosophy is… "As within, so without, as above, so below, as the universe, so the soul." This philosophical perspective outlines the idea that who we are on the inside will be created in the world around us.

In "Awakening the Light Within: Your Journey to 5th Dimension Expansion in 2024," we will explore the various aspects of this profound shift and provide practical resources, meditations, and guidance to support your personal transformation. Together, let us embrace the divine light within us and create a new reality of love, harmony, and unity on Earth.

Characteristics of the 5th Dimension

As we embark on our journey to 5th dimensional expansion in 2024, it is important to understand the characteristics that define this higher dimension. The 5th dimension is a realm of higher consciousness, where love, unity, and enlightenment prevail. It is a state of being that transcends the limitations of the physical world and offers boundless opportunities for growth and spiritual awakening.

One of the key characteristics of the 5th dimension is the presence of unconditional love. In this dimension, love is not limited to personal relationships but extends to all beings and the entire universe. Light workers, healers, way-showers, and awakening souls are familiar with the power of love and its ability to heal, transform, and uplift. In the 5th dimension, love is the foundation of all interactions and decisions, creating harmony and unity among individuals.

Another characteristic of the 5th dimension is the understanding and acceptance of oneness. In this dimension, there is a deep awareness that we are all interconnected and part of a larger cosmic tapestry. Light workers, healers, and awakened souls have experiences of this interconnectedness and are actively working towards creating a more compassionate and inclusive world. In the 5th dimension, this understanding becomes the norm, leading to the emergence of a global community based on cooperation, collaboration, and mutual respect.

Enlightenment and spiritual growth are integral aspects of the 5th dimension. As we expand into this realm, we tap into our inner wisdom and connect with our higher selves. Light workers, healers, and awakening souls are already on a path of self-discovery and spiritual awakening, and the 5th dimension offers a deeper level of understanding and connection. In this dimension, we can access higher states of consciousness, experience profound insights, and manifest our true potential.

Our journey to 5th dimension in 2024 is an invitation to embrace the characteristics of this higher realm and return to our original blueprint of 12 Chakras fully operational and in harmony with the divine. These Chakras are already available to us, and in 2024 we will upgrade and raise our vibrations to allow these energy centers to be accessible to us all. We will discuss this further in Chapter 3.

The Importance of 5th Dimensional Expansion

In the ever-evolving landscape of spirituality and personal growth, the concept of 5th dimensional expansion has gained immense significance. As awakening souls, we are being called to embark on a profound journey of self-discovery and transformation. The year 2024 holds tremendous potential for Your 5th dimensional expansion, so embrace this path and allow the light to shine and guide you.

We ask the question 'How do we expand?'

Our 'soul-self' separates from the Divine Creator of All to experience life in all forms. We create a conscious simulation/version of ourselves in order to have the experience of forgetting who we truly are, so that we can discover who we are from a new perspective.

The structure of existence never changes. Our relationship to it, our experiences and perspectives of it are constantly changing. This is how expansion occurs on all dimensions, in all directions, through time and space.

In this expansion process the movement of our Energy, our Life Force is essential. Moving energy in our body and within our etheric bodies is where expansion occurs also. When we eat, we move energy in our body through the processing, absorbing and eliminating of food – same as thoughts and feelings. In our body our kidneys are the main generators of the life force (Chi energy), they are also said to energetically represent our feelings and emotions. We recommend drinking plenty of 'structured water' as this can be programmed with your intentions and with crystals to raise your vibration. Here is a FREE information pdf on how to make Crystal Elixirs.

Understanding the 5th dimension is crucial. Unlike the limited and dense 3rd-dimensional reality we have been accustomed to, the 5th dimension represents a higher vibrational plane of existence. It is a realm of expanded consciousness, where we experience a shift in our perception, thoughts, emotions, and actions. We become more attuned to our intuition, accessing higher wisdom and guidance. Our ability to manifest our desires amplifies, as we align with the energetic flow of the universe.

The significance of 5th dimension expansion lies in the profound transformation it brings to our lives. As we align with this higher frequency, Relationships become more harmonious, and our capacity for compassion, forgiveness, and empathy deepens. Our physical, emotional, and spiritual well-being improves, as we release old patterns, traumas, and limitations that no longer serve us.

Moreover, 5th dimension expansion is not just an individual journey but a collective one. As we expand into this higher dimension, we become catalysts for positive change in the world. Our presence, energy, and actions inspire others to awaken and embark on their own journey of growth and transformation.

We are way-showers, guiding others towards greater love, unity, and consciousness. By collectively expanding into the 5th dimension, we contribute to the healing and evolution of humanity, ultimately creating a more peaceful and enlightened world.

Your 5th dimension expansion in 2024 holds immense importance as it is a transformative journey that allows us to transcend limitations, tap into our divinity, and create positive change in the world. Get ready to embrace the profound transformation that awaits as you expand into the 5th dimension and step into your true power.

Chapter 2: Awakening to Your True Self

Embracing Your Authenticity

In the pursuit of spiritual growth and enlightenment, one must embrace their authenticity, for it is within the essence of our true selves that we find the key to unlocking our fullest potential. As awakened and awakening souls, we are all on a unique journey of raising our vibration to live with ease and grace within the 5th dimension. In 2024 this will be an easier and more profound journey than 2023. This chapter serves as a guide to help you navigate this transformative path and discover the power of embracing your authenticity.

Authenticity is the state of being true to oneself, and aligned with your deepest values, desires, and purpose. It involves peeling off the layers of societal conditioning, fears, and limiting beliefs that have kept us disconnected from our true selves. Embracing your authenticity is a radical act of self-love and self-acceptance, allowing you to shine your light brightly and radiate your unique gifts and talents. It is where your actions, values, and identity create a life that authentically reflects your genuine feelings and beliefs.

In the journey towards 5th dimensional expansion, embracing your authenticity is essential. The 5th dimension is a higher vibrational frequency that transcends the limitations of the 3rd dimension. This dimension is characterized by unity consciousness, unconditional love, and interconnectedness. To align with this frequency, we must shed the masks of conformity and step into our true selves. Aligning to our authentic self, enables us to embrace our uniqueness and let shine our true talents and our passions.

By embracing your authenticity, you not only empower yourself but also inspire others to do the same. Your authenticity becomes a beacon of light, guiding others towards their own self-discovery and expansion. It is through authenticity that we can create a ripple effect of positive change in the world and contribute to the collective awakening. When holding our vibration high, our energy radiates out into the world and the 'Law of attraction' brings back to you those people and situations that are vibrating at your level.

Practicing authenticity requires self-awareness, self-compassion, and a willingness to confront the shadows that lie within. It involves embracing your strengths, weaknesses, and vulnerabilities, and honouring them as integral parts of your being. It also entails trusting your intuition and following your heart's desires, even when they defy societal norms or expectations.

Remember, your soul's journey within the 5th dimension is not about conforming or fitting into a mold. It is about embracing the unique expression of your soul and allowing it to guide you towards your highest potential. Embracing your authenticity is a lifelong practice, as it requires continuous self-reflection, growth, and alignment with your soul's purpose. In the following chapters, I have offered some suggestions, resources, and practices to support you on your journey throughout 2024.

Embrace your uniqueness, celebrate your individuality, and let your light shine brightly, for it is through your authenticity that you will co-create a world filled with love, compassion, and unity.

Letting Go of Limiting Beliefs

In 2024, holding onto any limiting beliefs will inhibit on our journey towards expanding into the 5th dimension. Letting go, especially of those thoughts and experiences of 2023 that no longer serve us, will allow us to access transformation on a cellular level. As light workers, healers, and awakening souls, we have been called to transcend the boundaries of our old programming and embrace the infinite possibilities that await us in the higher dimensions.

Limiting beliefs are like shackles that bind us, preventing us from fully experiencing the magnificence of our true selves. These beliefs are often deeply ingrained in our subconscious minds, acquired through societal conditioning, past traumas, and negative experiences. They create a distorted lens through which we view ourselves and the world around us.

However, as we awaken to our divine nature, we realize that we are not bound by these limitations. We are powerful beings with the ability to create our reality. It is time to release the chains that hold us back and step into our full potential.

To let go of limiting beliefs, we must first identify them. Take a moment to reflect on the beliefs that have held you back in the past. Are you constantly telling yourself that you are not good enough? Do you believe that abundance is scarce and unattainable? Recognize these thoughts for what they are – illusions created by your egoic mind. In the 5th dimension, scarcity and lack are replaced by abundance and prosperity, allowing each individual to flourish and thrive.

Once you have identified your limiting beliefs, it is essential to challenge them. Ask yourself, "Is this belief true? Does it serve my highest good?" Often, you will find that these beliefs are based on fear and lack, rather than truth and abundance. Replace these limiting beliefs with empowering ones that align with your divine essence.

I have found that working with ThetaHealing™ is one of the best ways to transform these limiting beliefs combined with affirmations and 'tapping'. This is where you 'tap' your body in a specific way, to release your unconscious beliefs that are stored in your body from a very young age and often connected to your past life limiting beliefs brought to this life to transform. As we move further into our 5th dimensional bodies, we can no longer hold these lower vibrations and we no longer will experience Karma, as is the divine plan. There is a Free downloadable pdf on my webpage on the 'Introduction to Tapping'. www.caraelliotthealinghouse.com/selfdevelopment

Letting go of limiting beliefs requires consistent practice and self-compassion. It is a process that takes time and patience. Surround yourself with supportive individuals who uplift and inspire you. Engage in activities that nourish your soul and expand your consciousness. As a Soul Coach and Light Language Activator, I offer a variety of modalities of healing and transformation to support you on your Soul's Journey in 2024.

Remember, dear light workers, healers, way-showers, and awakening souls, you are here to create a new reality. By letting go of limiting beliefs, you open yourself up to the infinite possibilities that the 5th dimension holds. Embrace the journey of self-discovery and expansion, for it is through releasing the old that we make way for the new. Trust in your divine essence and know that you are capable of creating a reality beyond your wildest dreams.

Connecting with Your Higher Self

"The greatest spiritual secret in the world is that every problem has a spiritual solution, not because every prayer is answered by a higher power, but because the true self, once discovered, is the source of creativity, intelligence and personal growth. No external solution has such power. The true self is the basis for being deeply optimistic about how life turns out and who you really are, behind the screen of doubt and confusion. The path to it isn't simply inspiring; it's the source of solutions that emerge from within."
Deepak Chopra, MD

As light workers, healers, way-showers, and awakening souls, one of the most profound and transformative experiences on our journey to 5th dimension expansion in 2024 is the connection with our 'true self' our higher self. This connection serves as a guiding light, a source of wisdom, and a doorway to our true essence.

The higher self, also known as the soul or the divine aspect of our being, is the part of us that exists beyond the limitations of the physical body and the ego. It is eternal, limitless, and connected to the universal consciousness. When we connect with our higher self, we tap into a wellspring of knowledge, love, and guidance that can help navigate our path towards self-realization and spiritual growth.

To connect with our higher self, we must first create a space of stillness and inner silence. This can be achieved through meditation, deep breathing exercises, or simply finding a quiet place in nature. As we quiet the mind and release the distractions of the external world, we create an opening for our higher self to make its presence known.

Once we have cultivated this inner stillness, we can start to establish a dialogue with our higher self. This can be done through journaling, automatic writing, or engaging in inner conversations. By asking questions and listening for the subtle whispers of our higher self, we can gain insight into our life purpose, soul contracts, and the lessons we are here to learn.

This brings us to the question of 'How can we tell the difference between my ego/personality voice and my higher self (intuition)?'

Being aware of all the voices in your mind is challenging but also crucial on the path to enlightenment. As we progress on our spiritual journeys, there is a time when we want to learn the difference between ego and intuition. Before we sharpen our higher senses, these two voices may be challenging to distinguish.

Intuition is more like a message than a messenger. It guides you in the moment to help you make decisions that will have a positive impact on your overall human experience. Intuition is connected to spirit guides in the sense that intuitive information usually follows your life plan.

As we awaken spiritually, we become more aware of the ego voice. As a result, we may feel surprised to learn the degree to which it runs our decisions. Thus, we enter the stage of discernment. Discernment gives us an opportunity to choose to either **Respond** (trusting our inner guidance) or to **React** (ego/personality).

Connecting with our higher self also requires trust and surrender. We must let go of the need for control and allow our higher self to guide us on our journey. This can be challenging, as the ego often seeks to maintain a sense of control and certainty. However, by surrendering to the wisdom and guidance of our higher self, we open ourselves up to infinite possibilities and a deeper sense of purpose.

As we deepen our connection with our higher self, we may experience profound shifts in our consciousness and perception of reality. We may find ourselves more aligned with our authentic selves, making choices that are in alignment with our soul's purpose. We may also develop a greater sense of compassion, love, and interconnectedness with all beings.

One way to practice this in meditations or vision boarding is instead of telling the Universe what you want, tell the universe you are open to receive your vision directly from the divine to your higher self. Then focus on the feelings of your future rather than the specifics of material desires.
In this approach, you create a space for delightful surprises as your destiny unfolds.

In 2024 cultivating stillness, establishing a regular dialogue with your higher self, and surrendering to its guidance, we can tap into the infinite wisdom and love that resides within us. Embracing this connection allows us to awaken the light within and embark on a transformative journey towards self-realization and spiritual growth.

Cultivating Self-Acceptance and Self-Love

In 2024 the path of self-acceptance and self-love becomes essential. As light workers, healers, way-showers, and awakening souls, we understand the significance of inner transformation and the power it holds in creating a better world. However, often in our pursuit of helping others and raising the collective consciousness, we tend to overlook the importance of nurturing our own souls.

What is Self-love?

Self-love is a state of appreciation for yourself that grows from actions that support our physical, psychological and spiritual growth.
It means having a high regard for your own wellbeing and happiness, taking care of your own needs and not sacrificing your wellbeing to please others.

Foundations Self-Acceptance and Self-Love in your life

- Self Care – taking action of a practice that you engage in to take care of your physical, emotional, mental and spiritual wellbeing.
- Self Awareness – is the ability to recognise and understand your own thoughts, feelings, emotions, and behaviors.
- Self Acceptance - recognising, embracing, and being honoring your own strengths, weaknesses, values, and beliefs.
- Self-Compassion - treating yourself with kindness, warmth, and understanding in times of suffering, difficulty, or failure. Self-talk that is encouraging.
- Self Esteem – having confidence in your own worth, value, and abilities. Holding positive opinions of yourself, such as I AM worthy, I AM loved.

CARAELLIOTTHEALINGHOUSE.COM

Self-Acceptance is a vital aspect of our personal evolution. It is the ability to acknowledge and embrace all parts of ourselves – the light and the shadow. By accepting ourselves fully, we can heal wounds, release limiting beliefs, and let go of the need for external validation. Only then can we truly step into our power and embrace the transformational journey towards the 5th dimension.

When we are able to accept ourselves, light and shadow aspects, the self-love follows.

Self-love is not selfish; it is a positive prerequisite for our growth and the ability to support others effectively. It is about recognizing our worthiness, embracing our flaws, and honoring and respecting our unique journey. When we truly accept and love ourselves, we radiate a higher vibration that attracts positive experiences and empowers us to manifest our desires.

To cultivate self-love and acceptance, we must begin by prioritizing our self-care. This involves setting boundaries, honoring our needs, and engaging in practices that nourish our mind, body, and heart and soul. Whether it is through meditation, energy healing, journaling, or engaging in creative activities, finding moments of solitude and self-reflection allows us to reconnect with our true essence.

Furthermore, practicing self-compassion is crucial. We must learn to treat ourselves with kindness, forgiveness, and understanding, just as we would with a dear friend. By shifting our inner dialogue from self-criticism to self-compassion, we create a nurturing environment for growth and transformation. Thus, demonstrating to those around us that, that it is possible to change and expand our awareness / consciousness to raise our vibration to the 5th dimensional frequencies.

Surrounding ourselves with a supportive community is also necessary on this journey. Connecting with like-minded individuals who understand our spiritual path and can offer guidance and encouragement can be transformative. By seeking out mentors, attending workshops, or joining online forums, we can find the support and inspiration needed to cultivate self-love and acceptance. HealingHouse with Cara offers a variety of workshops and online courses.

CARAELLIOTTHEALINGHOUSE.COM

Chapter 3: Navigating the Ascension Process

Recognizing Ascension Symptoms

Ascension symptoms are the body's response to the increasing vibrational frequencies and the energetic shifts that occur during the awakening process. These symptoms can manifest in different ways, and while they may vary from person to person, there are some common experiences that many individuals go through in 2024.

For those of you who having been doing the inner work and living in the higher frequencies you will ride the wave of energy as it rolls into the planet.. it has started... you will feel more at peace as it elevates your frequency even more. You may only experience some of these symptoms for short periods of time. Know that this is a tune up and alignment of your energy to your higher self and the universal energy from Source, Creator of All.

Those who are still needing to do their inner work will experience a lot of realizations, instant awakenings, and instant coming online of your 'spiritual gifts'. You will 'see' and become more aware. Your physical experiences will vary depending on where you are on your soul's journey.

One of the most common physical symptoms of ascension is fatigue or exhaustion. As your body adjusts to the higher frequencies, it requires more rest and downtime to integrate the new energies. You may find yourself needing more sleep or feeling drained even after a full night's rest. It is essential to honor your body's needs and give yourself permission to rest reflect and recharge.

Another physical manifestation of ascension is experiencing various aches and pains. These can range from headaches and joint pain to muscle soreness and tingling sensations. These discomforts often occur due to the release of old energy patterns and the recalibration of your physical body to accommodate higher levels of light. It is essential to listen to your body and provide it with the necessary care and support it needs during this process.

Emotionally, ascension symptoms can manifest as mood swings, heightened sensitivity, and increased emotional intensity. You may find yourself feeling more emotional than usual, experiencing waves of joy, sadness, anger, or even a sense of detachment. It is important to acknowledge and honour these emotions without judgment and allow them to flow through you. Emotional release and healing practices, such as meditation, journaling, or seeking support from a trusted friend or energy healer, can be beneficial during this time.

Energetically, you may experience heightened intuition, psychic abilities, or a stronger connection to your higher self and spiritual guidance. This can manifest as vivid dreams, synchronicities, increased intuition, or a deep sense of knowing. Embrace these gifts and explore ways to further develop and expand your spiritual abilities.

These high vibrational energies are contagious and the people and environments that you surround yourself with have a significant impact on your own energy and well-being. It's important to choose your company and environment wisely as you will become something closely resembling your surroundings and the people around you. Set boundaries and cultivate positivity and nurturing relationships and surroundings in order to create a space for growth and happiness.

Sensitive empaths absorb everything. If you surround yourself with positivity, you will absorb and reflect positivity. Similarly, if you are around negative people or in a negative environment, you will be infected and affected in compromising ways.

Note: This light that has being flooding the planet since December 2023, has created a huge and profound elevation of energy for humanity. A New Earth is forming. A new way of being. This energy will lay the foundations and anchor into the earth, to build the template for the Golden Age of Gaia (as it was for Atlantis).

There is abundance of high frequency streaming into our planet, even as I write this book. It is detected and recorded by the Schuman resonance radars which pick up the solar waves of energy coming from our sun. These high frequencies are from the 5th and 6th dimensions. They are coming from the galactic center where the higher energy beings are here to help us raise our vibration to become our own sovereign beings.

As the all planets are direct (from January -April 2024), this gives a clearer path for the high frequency energy to align with our higher self to upgrade and raise our vibration to expand into our 5th dimensional bodies.

All the aches and pains we may experience are our physical and light bodies aligning to receive this upgrade. As the light comes in and purges and then calm energy in our bodies. New timelines are emerging to allow us access to these higher dimensions.

The timelines have been merging or breaking away especially since 2020. This has been setting up the framework for us to access the higher streams of energy. A new age is dawning this year.

So how do we anchor this high vibration?

We do this by anchoring the source light through our bodies to the earth through our Earth Star Chakra. Reclaim your own power, be totally centred in the love and joy of being you. Allow your mind to be calm and peaceful and bless your body with appreciation, kindness and love.

Remember to stand strong in your own truth and embrace your self-esteem and self-acceptance. Do your best not to compromise your values and live by the truth of your own beliefs. When you treat yourself with love and respect and dignity, you are standing in alignment with the universal life force energy of Love and Light.

The journey towards 5th dimension expansion in 2024 is a transformative and profound experience. Recognizing and understanding the symptoms associated with ascension will not only help you navigate through this process with more grace and ease but also empower you to fully embrace and integrate the higher frequencies of light. Remember to be gentle with yourself, practice self-care, and seek support from your spiritual community as you embark on this transformative journey of awakening the light within.

Balancing Your Energy Centres

In your quest for spiritual growth and personal transformation, balancing your energy centres is of utmost importance. As light workers, healers, way-showers, and awakening souls, you are on a profound journey towards expanding your consciousness and reaching the fifth dimension in 2024. This subchapter serves as a guide to help you navigate through this transformative process and align your energy centres for optimal spiritual, emotional, and physical well-being.

The body's energy is contained within Chakras – these energy centres are vital for the free flow of energy throughout our being. Each of the energy centres (Chakras) of the body correspond to specific aspects of our existence, such as our physical health, emotions, communication, intuition, and spiritual connection. When these energy centres are balanced and harmonized, we experience a sense of wholeness, vitality, and spiritual alignment.

There are seven major chakras according to ancient Sanskrit Philosophy. (The chakra system originated in India between 1500 and 500 BC in the oldest texts called the Vedas). However, since 2012 our 'Higher Chakras' have become activated and continue to open as we expand into our 5th dimensional bodies. All 12 Chakras need to be open an activated to be receptive to the higher dimensional frequencies and to maintain our vibration within the 4th and 5th dimensions.

In Sanskrit Chakra translates to "wheel" or "disk" and those who can see them describe the chakra centres as spinning wheels of light. Chakras are our energy centres that connect to our aura and dimensional light bodies.

In this book we will explore the seven major chakras and the 8th Higher Chakra - Earth Star Chakra, one of the five 'Higher' Chakras. There are also hundreds of minor and supporting chakras in the body.

The other 'Higher' Chakras (Earth, Core, and Soul Star Chakras, High Heart Chakra, Casual Chakra, and Stella Gateway) are explored in detail in my Advanced Crystal Healing online Certificate Course. Included in this advanced course are exercises and activities to protect your energies, and crystal healing meditations.

To begin balancing your energy centres, it is crucial to develop a deep understanding of your Aura and each chakra and its associated qualities. This knowledge empowers you to identify any imbalances or blockages that may hinder your spiritual growth. Through meditation, visualization, and energy healing practices, you can gradually restore harmony to your energy centers.

Balancing your energy centres

Start by grounding yourself, connecting with the Earth's energy, and focusing on your root chakra, located at the base of your spine. This chakra governs your sense of stability, security, and connection to the physical world. Visualise a vibrant red energy flowing into this chakra, clearing any stagnant energy, and bringing a renewed sense of grounding and stability.

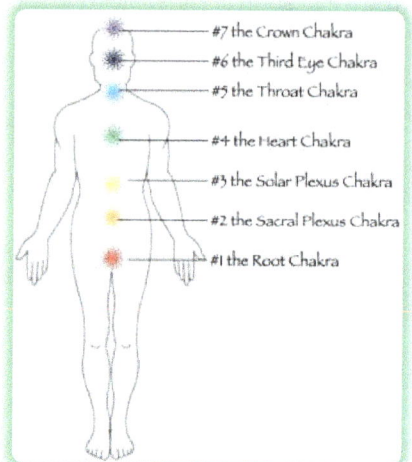

Visualise sending this light down to your Earth Star Chakra, which sits dimensional below your feet (6inches) into the earth. The Earth Star Chakra is essential to 'opening' the higher Chakras which then allows us to access the higher dimensions, in particular the 5th dimension. We cannot receive messages and connect to our Soul Star Chakra unless we are grounded through the Earth Star Chakra.

Moving up your 'spiritual backbone', the sacral chakra, located in the lower abdomen, governs your creativity, sexuality, and emotional well-being. Visualize a warm, orange light filling this chakra, releasing any emotional blockages and fostering a sense of joy, passion, and sensuality.

Next, focus on your solar plexus chakra, located in the upper abdomen, which governs your personal power, self-confidence, and manifestation abilities. Visualize a bright yellow light enveloping this chakra, igniting your inner fire and empowering you to step into your authenticity and personal power.

Continue this process, working with each chakra - the heart, throat, third eye, and crown - visualizing their respective colours and qualities, and bringing balance and harmony to each energy center. For more information on Chakras and Auras download the FREE pdf on my website.

To amplify your chakra clearing and balancing use crystals that are associated with each chakra. These easy-to-use online courses will give you an excellent understanding of crystals and crystal healing. To begin with, find crystals that match the colour of your chakras and use these when meditating. Further in this book we will explore high vibrational crystals that will amplify the expansion process and can be used in energy healing.

Balancing your energy centres is an ongoing practice. It requires self-awareness, inner work, and a commitment to your spiritual growth. As you cultivate this balance, you will experience a deeper connection to your higher self, enhanced intuition, and a greater capacity to manifest your desires. You will experience more balance in your life and therefore attract more of the same.
Remember the Law of Attraction - what energy you vibrate out into the world, you attract similar vibrations.

In 2024 - 2026 as our planet receives more upgrading energy, we need to clear and balance and upgrade our energy centres to receive and assimilate this high vibrational energy. Remember that balancing your energy centres is a vital component of your spiritual evolution no matter what year it is. Embrace this practice of chakra clearing and balancing regularly, and allow the light within you to shine brightly, illuminating your path and guiding you towards the transformation and expansion that awaits you.

Clearing and Releasing Past Traumas

As light workers, healers, way-showers, and awakening souls on the path to your 5th dimensional expansion in 2024, it is crucial to address the deep-seated wounds and traumas that may still be holding you back from reaching your highest potential. This subchapter will guide you on the transformative journey of clearing and releasing past traumas, allowing you to fully embody the radiant light within you.

In the process of awakening, it is common to uncover layers of unresolved emotions and experiences that have shaped our lives. These past traumas can be subtle or deeply ingrained, affecting our thoughts, emotions, relationships, and overall well-being. However, by acknowledging their presence and actively working towards healing, you can break free from their grip and step into the expansive realms of the 5th dimension.

As we begin the journey in 2024, so the clearing and cleansing continues... and old emotions or traumas rise to be seen, so they serve us if we feel them, as opportunities to feel. But this is not always easy. Acknowledge, accept, surrender, and heal away unwanted patterns. It is time to create new patterns that serve your heart and soul. Then pay attention to any loving feelings or thoughts that guide you to take action. Choose to act not react.

When trauma happens there is a 'soul fragmentation' that occurs, where a part of the soul or psyche stays in that place and that moment in time. It is 'stuck' on repeat in that emotion of the past, attracting situations of the same frequency and vibration. This can be a past life trauma or this life trauma. *I have found that Soul Hypnotherapy was successful for me to clear these past life 'stuck' traumas through time and space and through all dimensions.*

Buried deep in our subconscious we often act on auto pilot and not realize it is happening quietly in the background. So, we need to find the trauma and unresolved emotions and release it to change the frequency. This is the same for anything, whether we want to heal dis – ease, abuse patterns, limiting beliefs or we want to attract more of something, more abundance more joy etc.

At the same time, we also need to hold the vibration of 'acceptance' and be fully present with 'what is' and find the joy in the present moment (with intention). We can do this start by affirming each day and having gratitude in this moment. We are then asking to expand our vibration as well, so we are looking to clear the trauma / unresolved emotions that block us, the trauma that stops us from expanding and experiencing more.

It is essential to cultivate self-awareness and compassion. Big problems can be solved in small steps, when you are still and calm within your mind, the gentle voice from within will guide you through your processes. Listen carefully and you will hear the universal voice communicating through your heart. Remember to say a little prayer or affirmation and let Source, God, the Universal life force, take the burden of worry from your heart. Be patient, be peaceful, be calm. The problem will dissolve, and it will be resolved so you can evolve/ascend.

Just because you cannot see Angels or your guides, doesn't mean they are not there.

Take time to reflect on your past experiences and identify any traumas that still hold power over you. Remember, this is not about reliving or rehashing painful memories, but rather acknowledging and honoring the emotions that arise. Allow yourself to feel and release them in a safe and supportive environment. You may seek the support of an experienced energy healer or counsellor to support in this part of your journey.

Next, embrace the power of forgiveness. Forgiveness is not about condoning or forgetting the past; rather, it is a conscious choice to release the burden of resentment and anger. By forgiving yourself and others involved, you create space for healing and transformation. Seek guidance from trusted healers or engage in forgiveness practices such as meditation or journaling to support this process.

Additionally, explore various healing modalities that resonate with you. These may include energy healing, sound therapy, breathwork, meditation, or working with plant medicines. Each modality offers unique approaches to clearing and releasing past traumas, allowing you to access the wisdom and light within.

Remember, this journey of clearing and releasing past traumas is not linear or instantaneous. It requires patience, self-love, and ongoing commitment. Surround yourself with a supportive community of fellow light workers and seek professional guidance when needed. Together, you can create a sacred space for healing, growth, and the expansion of your consciousness.

As you embark on this transformative journey, know that you are not alone. The universal Source of Love and Light supports your growth and healing. Your life holds infinite possibilities for as you expand into your 5th dimensional perspective on life. Embrace the light within you, release the shackles of the past, and step into a future filled with love, joy, and limitless potential. Focus on your blessings that will come into your life as you continue to work towards higher levels of consciousness.

Embracing the Power of Forgiveness

In our journey towards 5th dimensional expansion in 2024, one of the most transformative and empowering tools we can harness is the power of forgiveness. As light workers, healers, way-showers, and awakening souls, we understand the immense weight of carrying resentments, grudges, and past hurts. These negative emotions not only hinder our personal growth and spiritual progress but also block the flow of divine energy within us.

Forgiveness, on the other hand, is a profound act of liberation and healing. It is the key that unlocks the doors of our hearts, allowing us to release the chains that bind us to past pain and suffering. When we forgive, we not only free ourselves from the burden of resentment, but we also extend compassion and understanding to those who may have caused us harm.

The power of forgiveness lies in its ability to transmute negative energy into love and light. By choosing to forgive, we shift our perspective from victimhood to empowerment, from anger to compassion, and from fear to love. This transformative process allows us to reclaim our personal power and align ourselves with the higher frequencies of the 5th dimension.

Forgiveness is not about condoning or forgetting the actions of others; it is about releasing ourselves from the grip of the past. It is a conscious choice to let go of the emotional baggage that holds us back from experiencing true freedom and joy. When we forgive, we create space within us for love, joy, and abundance to flow effortlessly.

When we forgive we choose to let go of the 'hope that things in the past would | could be different'. We can't change the past and continuing to 'wish you/they had done something different or said something different' only keeps us looped in this cycle of negative feelings. When we let go of the *hope* that it can be different and accept that it has happened, we release ourselves from this cycle of feelings.

Practicing forgiveness is a journey, and it begins with ourselves. We must first forgive ourselves for any mistakes, regrets, or self-judgments that may be weighing us down. Self-forgiveness allows us to cultivate self-love and acceptance, which in turn radiates outwards and positively impacts our relationships with others.

As we embrace the power of forgiveness, we become beacons of light and love in the world. Our ability to forgive not only transforms our own lives but also inspires and guides others on their own journeys of healing and spiritual growth. By embodying forgiveness, we become catalysts for positive change, creating a ripple effect of love and healing that extends far beyond ourselves.

I highly recommend the Colin Tippings - Radical Forgiveness process which you can do yourself with guidance from the book and worksheets. (written and audio). Radical Forgiveness gives you a step-by-step instruction in what begins as a healing process and culminates in an entirely new way of living in the world. You can download the ebook and worksheets for FREE.

CARAELLIOTTHEALINGHOUSE.COM

In 2024 from January to April, as all planets in our universe 'go direct' (Astology) ie are "awake' and sending this frequency to our planet, let us remember the profound power of forgiveness. As light workers, healers, way-showers, and awakening souls, let us courageously choose forgiveness as a path to liberation, healing, and divine expansion. Together, we can create a world infused with love, compassion, and unity, where forgiveness becomes the cornerstone of our collective consciousness.

See also a couple of my favorite people for more information on astrology in 2024. Debra Silverman and Tiarnie Vidler

Chapter 4: Resources and Practices for 5th Dimensional Expansion

Cultivating Inner Peace and Connection

To experience the New Earth frequencies of the 5th dimension, we need the courage to shift our perspectives from the dense, linear 3rd dimension to the energies of kindness, joy and love of the 5th dimension. When we awaken our unique journey and our part in the ascension of humanity, we will realize who we truly are and claim our sovereignty in this evolutionary consciousness shift.

Finding moments of peace and connection will help us to be aware of our perspectives and utilise this time to change our perspectives. As light workers, healers, and awakening souls, it is crucial for us to prioritize self-care and nurture our spiritual growth. In this section will explore several powerful practices and resources to navigate the challenges of life and awaken our inner light.

Meditation

> *Buddha was once asked, "What do you gain from meditation?" He replied, "Absolutely nothing. But, please, let me tell you what I've lost."*
> *"ANGER, ANXIETY, DEPRESSION, INSECURITY, FEAR OF OLD AGE & DEATH."*

Meditation is a practice that has been embraced by various cultures and spiritual traditions for centuries. It is practiced around the world, to get us in touch with our inner selves and our spiritual self. Meditation is related to the evolution of human consciousness. ie the more we become aware of the 'reality' around us, the more we can progress forward in our lives.

The great Sages of our past found that by developing their inner awareness, profound and lasting changes came about.

The word "Meditation" simply means awareness. Whatever you do with awareness is meditation. "Watching your breath" is mediation; listening to the birds is mediation. Rocking is even a form of meditation. Buddhists have a 'moving meditation' where you are aware of your surroundings and where you are moving your body. Meditation does not just have to be sitting still.

As long as these activities are free from any other distraction to the mind, it is effective meditation.

When meditating where you are quieting your mind and tuning into the present moment, creates a space for self-reflection, inner peace, and connection to our higher selves. As we embark on our journey to 5th dimension expansion in 2024, meditation becomes an essential practice to align ourselves with the higher frequencies and energies of this new dimension.

For your meditations –

- Allow the Oneness, the New Earth energies, and your divine feminine and sacred masculine energies to resonate with the eternal harmony Source of Light. These frequencies already vibrate deep within you, meditating and allowing yourself to feel this energy will bring forth the familiar feelings. From this place of your Inner Sacred Space, inspiration and activations awaken within you and will flow forth.

- Begin with a heart opening mediation using Rose Quartz Crystal. Free 11min meditation - see my website or Spotify. There are two other crystal mediations you can enjoy also for Free. **For more information on other mediations available for purchase see** www.caraelliotthealinghouse.com

It is your time to awaken.

Breathe and awaken...

Mindfulness

Mindfulness, on the other hand, is a way of being fully present and engaged in the current moment, with an open and non-judgmental attitude. It involves bringing our intention and our attention to our thoughts, feelings, and sensations, as well as to the world around us. By practicing mindfulness, we become more aware of our thoughts and emotions, allowing us to respond to situations with clarity and compassion.

Consider engaging in new practices to learn various ways of mindfulness. From breathwork and visualization to mantra repetition and body scanning, these techniques will empower you to cultivate inner peace, strengthen your connection to your higher self, and awaken your inherent light.

Practice presence and observation – Whenever you can, become aware of the present moment – right here, right now – and simply observe it. Simply observe without thought. Set an alarm on your phone two or three times a day, or put a few signs around your home or work space with the word PRESENCE or NOW to remind you to make contact with the present moment right now.

Pay attention to your breath – This is a great way to become more present. Again, if you're new to this, set an alarm on your phone two or three times daily to practice. Or place your favourite crystal on your desk or in the kitchen, and whenever you look at this crystal, this is a reminder to take 3 deep breaths. Yoga/exercise – Undertake exercise in a self-observant way. Notice your breath, feel your bodily sensations, observe your thoughts. Stay present. Yoga will often create a space for mind, body, soul presence.

Both meditation and mindfulness provide numerous benefits to our well-being and spiritual growth. They help us reduce stress, anxiety, and depression, promoting emotional balance and mental clarity. These practices also enhance our ability to connect with our intuition and receive guidance from our higher selves, helping us navigate the complexities of our journey to the 5th dimension expansion.

> *In this time of global awakening and transformation, your intuition is your essential guide on the journey toward greater peace and awareness.*

As light workers, healers, and awaken souls, it is our responsibility to embark on this transformative journey with an open heart and mind. By embracing the practices of meditation and mindfulness, we can tap into our true potential, ignite our inner light, and radiate love and healing into the world. Together, let us embark on this journey of self-discovery, expansion, and awakening as we step into the 5th dimension in 2024.

Energy Healing Techniques

Energy healing is based on the principle that everything is energy, and the human body is an intricate web of energy fields. By understanding and working with these energy fields, we can restore balance, harmony, and well-being to our physical, mental, emotional, and spiritual bodies.

One of the most widely known energy healing techniques is Reiki, a Japanese practice that involves the channeling of universal life force energy through the practitioner's hands to the recipient. Reiki serves to clear energy blockages, promote relaxation, and enhance the body's natural healing abilities. I encourage you to find the Energy Healing that resonates with you the most. Other examples include; Crystal healing, Intuitive healing, ThetaHealing™, Light Language activations, chakra balancing and many more.

Another powerful technique is crystal healing, where specific crystals and gemstones are used to align, balance, and amplify the body's energy centers, known as chakras. Each crystal carries unique properties and vibrations that can assist in healing, protection, and spiritual growth.

Sound healing is yet another modality that utilizes the vibrational qualities of sound to restore harmony and balance within the body. Whether through the use of singing bowls, tuning forks, or chanting, the resonance of sound can penetrate deep into our cells, releasing stagnant energy and facilitating healing on multiple levels.

The ancient practice of acupuncture involves the insertion of fine needles into specific points along the body's meridian system. By stimulating these points, energy flow is restored, promoting physical and emotional well-being.

Moreover, I encourage you to explore the power of breathwork and meditation as energy healing techniques. Conscious breathing techniques can release trapped emotions, clear stagnant energy, and bring about a sense of calm and clarity. Meditation, on the other hand, allows us to connect with our inner selves, access higher states of consciousness, and tap into the limitless healing potential of the universe.

Remember, dear light workers, healers, way-showers, and awakening souls, your commitment to personal growth and healing is not only transforming your own life but also contributing to the collective consciousness shift towards a more enlightened and harmonious world. Embrace these energy healing techniques as powerful tools on your path to awakening the light within.

ANY ACTIVITY DONE WITH LOVE & PRESENCE IS A SPIRITUAL PRACTICE.

CARAELLIOTTHEALINGHOUSE.COM

Journaling and Self-Reflection

As we embark on a groundbreaking era, moving towards our spiritual expansion into our 5th dimensional bodies, the practice of journaling and self-reflection holds immense significance. For light workers, healers, and awakening souls, this section is dedicated to exploring the transformative power of journaling in facilitating personal growth, healing, and spiritual evolution.

Journaling, in its essence, is a sacred act of self-expression and self-discovery. It allows us to access the depths of our inner world, uncover hidden truths, and gain clarity on our emotions, thoughts, and experiences. Through journaling, we create a safe space for our authentic voice to be heard and witnessed, free from judgment or external influences. It becomes a mirror that reflects our innermost desires, fears, and aspirations, enabling us to gain profound insights into ourselves.

By engaging in regular journaling, we cultivate self-awareness and mindfulness. We learn to observe our patterns, triggers, and limiting beliefs, allowing us to release what no longer serves us and make space for growth and expansion. It also is work out problems, to laugh at ourselves, and sometimes cry if it's needed. It is an opportunity to have a creative outlet to express ourselves.

As light workers and healers, this self-reflection becomes essential in identifying our own areas of healing and growth, enabling us to better serve others on their own journeys.

Moreover, journaling serves as a powerful tool for manifestation and intention setting. By writing down our dreams, goals, and desires, we bring them into the physical realm, giving them substance and energy. Journaling allows us to formulate clear intentions and create a roadmap towards our 5th dimensional expansion in 2024. It is a co-creative process with the Source of All / the Universe, as we align our thoughts, words, and actions with our highest vision.

CARAELLIOTTHEALINGHOUSE.COM

If we want to know and feel success and fulfilment in our life, in our career, our relationships, our health, artistic endeavours, or making a contribution to the world around us, it takes some planning. We create a vision and a plan and allow the universe to provide opportunities in the directions we want to go. With journaling and creating a vision board, we can set our intentions and each day we look at the vision board or reread our journal we know what our reason and purpose for experiencing and living each day.

First you need to know what you want to create and why. Then you need a practical plan you can easily follow that spells out all the steps to get there. With map in hand, you know just the twists and turns to take you to your destination, so you don't get lost along the way.

Stick to your plans and priorities and keep your promises to yourself. Stay focused, stay positive, commit to your goals and dreams and to your heart's desires… your persistence will pay off. Your faith is stronger than your fears and doubts.

In addition to journaling, self-reflection practices enhance our connection to the divine and our inner wisdom. Through meditation, contemplation, and introspection, we create space for divine guidance and intuitive insights to emerge. We learn to listen to the whispers of our soul and gain clarity on our purpose and path.

Here are some ideas to help if you get stuck for 'starting phrases', in your writing.

Try some of these. Allow words to flow from your hands.

- If I could reclaim my life, I would…
- Today I feel…
- What I most want right now is…
- What I most need right now is…
- What I'm most afraid of is…
- I am grateful for…

Another way to journal is to give yourself a new journaling task to accomplish- so that you improve yourself as you learn new things.

Journaling can also be done with a partner if that is easier for you - ie. set a night & time when you set aside time together to do this journaling.

Further suggestions:

- Write every day. Even if you can only write 5 mins worth, each sitting.
- Write down your negative thoughts and allow them to be released. Then finish off with at least one thing that you're thankful for in life.
- Start a gratitude diary

Journaling and self-reflection become invaluable ways to navigate the waves of transformation that are happening in 2024. They allow us to integrate our experiences, heal past wounds, and align with our authentic selves. By embracing these practices, we empower ourselves to shine our light and become beacons of love, compassion, and transformation in the world.

Get ready to embark on a transformative journey of self-discovery, healing, and spiritual awakening. The light within you is ready to awaken, and the time for your expansion is now.

Sacred Rituals and Ceremony

In the journey of awakening and stepping into our 5th dimensional bodies, sacred rituals and ceremony play a crucial role in aligning our energies, connecting with our higher selves, and embracing the divine within. As light workers, healers, way-showers, and awakening souls, we understand the significance of these practices in nurturing our spiritual growth and evolution.

Sacred rituals are powerful as they allow us to create a sacred space, where we can connect with the divine energies and higher realms. They enable us to tune into the frequencies of love, harmony, and oneness, which are the essence of the 5th dimension. Through these rituals, we establish a deep connection with our inner self and the universal consciousness, facilitating the expansion of our spiritual awareness.

Ceremony, on the other hand, takes these sacred rituals to a higher level by infusing intention, symbolism, and reverence. It is a way to honor and celebrate the divine within and around us. Ceremonies provide a structured framework for our spiritual practices, allowing us to deepen our connection with the divine and integrate its wisdom into our daily lives.

These practices can include meditation, chanting, energy healing, crystal work, sacred dance, and sound therapy, among others. The key is to choose practices that resonate with our unique essence and align with our intentions for growth and transformation.

By engaging in these sacred practices, we create a vibrational shift within ourselves, clearing any lower energies, and raising our frequency to match the higher dimensions. We become conduits of divine light, love, and healing energy, enabling us to serve as beacons of hope and inspiration for others on their own journeys.

As light workers, healers, and way-showers, it is our responsibility to share our knowledge and experiences with others, guiding them towards their own 5th dimensional expansion. By incorporating sacred rituals and ceremony into our lives, we create a ripple effect of positive transformation, not only for ourselves but for the collective consciousness as well.

I encourage you to start up a meditation group or gathering of like-minded souls to come together to support and encourage each other in your learning and growth. Together the power of intention is far greater than the individual. Activities in nature together allows for genuine connection and a place where each of you can share your journey, ask questions, share resources and network. These gatherings can be online or in person.

Let us embrace the power of sacred rituals and ceremony, as we step into our 5th dimensional expansion in 2024. Together, we can awaken the light within and create a world filled with love, peace, and unity. May these practices guide us on our journey and inspire us to shine our light brightly, illuminating the path for others to follow.

Surrounding Yourself with Positivity

In the grand journey of awakening and expanding our consciousness, it is essential to recognize the power and influence of the environment we immerse ourselves in. As light workers, healers, way-showers, and awakening souls, we understand the significance of surrounding ourselves with positivity in order to navigate our path towards the 5th dimension expansion in 2024.

The energy that surrounds us plays a crucial role in shaping our thoughts, emotions, and overall well-being. By consciously choosing to fill our surroundings with positivity, we create a harmonious environment that supports our growth and transformation.

One of the most effective ways to surround ourselves with positivity is by organising our physical space. Our homes, workplaces, and personal sanctuaries should be filled with objects, colours, and scents that uplift our spirits and inspire us on our journey. Surrounding ourselves with vibrant artwork, calming crystals, and nature-inspired elements can create a sacred space that nurtures our souls and enhances our connection with the divine.

Beyond our physical surroundings, the people we choose to interact with also have a profound impact on our energy. It is crucial to surround ourselves with like-minded individuals who resonate with our higher aspirations and support our spiritual growth. Seek out the company of fellow light workers, healers, and way-showers who can provide guidance, share their wisdom, and inspire us on our path.

When choosing those in your life, make your decision based on the principles of your own truth. Trust your inner voice, your 'gut' feelings, it will always guide you through your decisions and send you in the right direction to meet the 'right people'. Trust – Believe – Receive

At times it can feel challenging find other individuals who share our expansion and ascension beliefs, so it's important to remember that we are strategically placed where we are for a higher purpose and reason. To share your light and to assist in the global ascension awakening on this beautiful planet we choose to incarnate onto.

As conduits and beacons of the light, our energy and our presence ripples out around you and spreads beyond your immediate surroundings. Coming together in groups for meditation and other 'spiritual' practices, amplifies this light and can be shared around the world. Networking with other light works, healers and awakened souls is an important part of our journey and we each have our unique roles in the collective awakening of humanity.

'Follow your own footsteps' - every journey begins with a single step.

In addition to our external environment, it is imperative to cultivate a positive inner landscape. This can be achieved through practices such as meditation, visualisation, and affirmation. By engaging in these activities regularly, we can cleanse our minds of negativity and align ourselves with higher frequencies. As we raise our own vibration, we naturally attract positive experiences and opportunities that contribute to our 5th dimension expansion.

Finally, it is essential to be mindful of the information and media we consume. In today's digital age, we are bombarded with endless streams of news, social media, and entertainment. Being discerning about what we allow into our awareness is crucial. Seek out sources of inspiration, knowledge, and positivity that uplift and empower us. By consciously choosing what we expose our minds to, we can maintain a state of positivity and keep our focus aligned with our journey towards 5th dimension expansion.

Surrounding ourselves with positivity is a fundamental aspect of our journey. By organising our physical space, choosing our company wisely, cultivating a positive inner landscape, and being mindful of the information we consume, we create an environment conducive to our spiritual growth. As light workers, healers, and awakening souls, let us embrace the power of positivity and create a world that resonates with the frequency of love, light, and unity.

Connecting with Nature and the Elements

In our fast-paced, modern world, it is easy to become disconnected from the natural world and the elements that surround us. However, as light workers, healers, way-showers, and awakening souls, it is essential for us to reconnect with nature and the elements in order to fully embrace our journey to 5th dimension expansion in 2024.

Nature has a profound ability to heal, nurture, and guide us on our spiritual path. By immersing ourselves in the beauty of the natural world, we can tap into the wisdom and energy that it holds. Whether it is taking a walk in the forest, sitting by the ocean, or simply observing a sunrise, these experiences allow us to align with the rhythms of the Earth and the universe.

The elements - earth, water, air, and fire - are also integral to our spiritual growth and transformation. Each element holds its own unique qualities and lessons that can assist us in our journey.

Earth represents stability, grounding, and abundance. By connecting with the earth element, we can find a sense of security and balance in our lives.

Water symbolizes emotions, intuition, and healing. By spending time near bodies of water, such as lakes or rivers, we can cleanse and purify our emotions, allowing us to flow more freely in our spiritual journey.

Air represents communication, clarity, and inspiration. By spending time in open spaces, such as parks or mountains, we can breathe in fresh air and gain mental clarity, helping us to connect with our higher selves and receive guidance from the divine.

Fire symbolizes transformation, passion, and creativity. By sitting around a campfire or lighting candles, we can harness the energy of fire to ignite our inner spark and bring our dreams and desires to life.

Connecting with nature and the elements not only benefits us individually but also contributes to the collective consciousness and the awakening of humanity. As we deepen our connection with the natural world, we become more attuned to the needs of the Earth and are inspired to take action to protect and preserve it for future generations.

Create your own path. Listen to your inner voice and learn from rivers, trees, rocks, and crystals. Feel the presence of the rocks, earth, mountains, streams, and lakes. Don't just gaze upon them, let yourself feel what they are like in their parts and as a whole. Feel the openness of the sky, feel its moods, its peace and its rage, and its calming infinite nighttime beauty. Notice how the spirit of the sky feels for you.

Honor each of these and honor each other. Honor Morther Earth and honor the Great Spirit – the Source of All. Honor yourself and all of Creation.

CARAELLIOTTHEALINGHOUSE.COM

By immersing ourselves in the beauty of nature and aligning with the energies of the elements, we can tap into the wisdom, healing, and transformation that they offer. Let us honor and cherish the natural world as we continue to awaken the light within and create a brighter future for all.

Using High Vibrational Crystals

Crystals have long been revered for their metaphysical properties and healing abilities. In the journey towards 5th dimension expansion, these precious gemstones become even more powerful tools for light workers, healers, way-showers, and awakening souls. Harnessing the energy of high vibrational crystals can greatly enhance spiritual growth, amplify intentions, and facilitate the awakening process.

High vibrational crystals are those that resonate with the frequencies of the higher realms, allowing us to connect with our higher selves and the divine source more effortlessly. These crystals possess an energy that is purer, more refined, and aligned with the frequencies of love, truth, and light. As we move towards 5th dimension expansion in 2024 -2026, the energetic support provided by these crystals becomes even more essential.

Some crystals have a much more powerful effect on you and your environment than others. Crystals do have vibrations. Low-frequency crystals are calming and work well to soothe the mind and emotions. High-vibration crystals give you more energy, uplift your spirit, and have much more intense metaphysical and spiritual healing properties.

One such crystal is Clear Quartz, known as the "master healer" due to its ability to amplify intentions and purify energies. Clear quartz can assist in clearing blockages, enhancing clarity and focus, and facilitating spiritual growth. Its high vibrational nature makes it a perfect ally in the journey to 5th dimension expansion.

Amethyst, with its calming and protective properties, is another powerful crystal to work with during this transformative time. It can help to awaken intuition, deepen meditation experiences, and create a sense of peace and tranquility. Amethyst's connection to the higher realms makes it a valuable tool for light workers and awakening souls on their path to 5th dimension expansion.

Spirit Quartz, also known as cactus quartz or fairy quartz. It holds the energy of purification, balance, evolution and best used on the crown chakra. Spirit quartz is a master healer and can be used to balance the chakras and energies. The unique part of spirit quartz is it works well on groups of people and families facilitating bonding and strengthening ties. It assists in relieving negative attachments. This is a gentle crystal and is used to assist in transitions especially with souls facing death or terminal illnesses as it eases release and gives protection for the journey. There is something truly magical and spiritual about this crystal.

Rose Quartz, the stone of unconditional love, is an essential crystal for healing and heart-centered growth. Its gentle energy promotes self-love, compassion, and emotional healing, allowing for the release of old wounds and the embracing of divine love. Rose quartz supports the integration of higher vibrations and assists in aligning with the frequencies of the 5th dimension.

Lemurina Seed Crystal, also known as Lemurian Quartz is a popular choice for healers, grid workers, way-showers and spiritual teachers. These Lemurian crystals connect you with ancient wisdom, Source energy and the higher dimensions. They also help you release fear and shine your light.

Other high vibrational crystals that can aid in the journey to 5th dimension expansion include selenite, labradorite, and moldavite. Each crystal carries its unique energetic signature, offering specific benefits and guidance on the spiritual path.

Are you interested to gain a unique in depth understanding about Crystals, their energy and how to use them in everyday life? If so, I encourage you to join my community of crystal enthusiasts who have either attended my in-person courses or my online crystal healing courses. Understanding 'The energies of crystals' and their physical and metaphysical properties, you will develop your own 'healer potential'.

In these courses you will be able to use crystals to balance your chakras, cleanse & harmonise your living/working space and choose one for everyday use. You will learn practical crystal healing methods developed by a professional crystal healing practitioner. The courses offer you practical, experiential and instructional-based knowledge that you can only get from interactive learning.

Choosing, Clearing and Cleansing your Crystals

When choosing your high vibrational crystals, setting your intention for the reason for selecting the crystal is important. My best advice is to allow the crystal to choose you. When you look at crystals, which one appeals to you? Which draw your attention? If you have the opportunity to hold and touch the crystals, which one feels 'right' to you or feels different.

When working with high vibrational crystals, it is important to cleanse and charge them regularly to maintain their optimum energetic properties. If protective stones store too much external energy, then they can lose their effectiveness for healing. Cleansing your crystals can be done in various ways such as moonlight, sunlight, sound, sage and intention. By attuning to the crystals' energy and incorporating them into daily practices like meditation, affirmation, or energy healing, their transformative power can be harnessed to support your 5th dimensional expansion in 2024.

It's also important to cleanse crystals immediately after buying them or receiving as a gift. They have been handled by many people, leaving energetic imprints on their journey to you. They also need to be cleansed after wearing it, and whenever you use it for healing purposes. The clearing methods are also a part of our process of connection and communion with our crystals.

What determines whether these methods work for you is your belief system and your intention? There are many methods that will work; it is up to you to find those that feel most effective to you. Remember that you are offering a clearing not imposing it. There are many more options for cleansing your crystals.

On my website I have a resource for how to 'Use your crystals', which outlines many ways to cleanse your crystals. Go to my website www.caraelliotthealinghouse.com/crystals and download the pdf as a resource for yourself.

Remember, as a light worker, healer, way-shower, or awakening soul, you have chosen to be here at this momentous time of collective awakening. Utilizing the wisdom and energetic support of high vibrational crystals can greatly enhance your journey and assist in anchoring the light within yourself and the world.

Embrace the power of these sacred gemstones and allow them to guide you towards your 5th dimension expansion during 2024 - 2026.

Chapter 5:
Stepping into Your Lightworker Role

Recognizing the Interconnectedness of All Beings

On this extraordinary journey of life, there is a profound truth that lies at the core of our being - the interconnectedness of all beings. As light workers, healers, way-showers, and awakening souls, we are called to awaken to this truth and embrace it with open hearts and minds. This understanding is essential as we embark on our journey to 5th dimension expansion in 2024.

The concept of interconnectedness goes beyond our human understanding. It transcends the boundaries of time, space, and individuality. It reminds us that every being, from the tiniest insect to the tallest tree, from the distant stars to the depths of the ocean, is connected in a magnificent web of energy. We are all threads woven intricately together, each playing a unique role in the grand symphony of life.

When we recognize this interconnectedness, we realize that our thoughts, words, and actions have a ripple effect that extends far beyond our immediate surroundings. Every choice we make, every intention we set, reverberates throughout the collective consciousness. We become aware of the immense power we possess to create positive change and transformation.

As we journey towards 5th dimension expansion in 2024, it is crucial to cultivate a deep sense of compassion and empathy for all beings. We must honor the sacredness of all life, treating every creature and every element of nature with reverence and respect. By doing so, we align ourselves with the divine flow of energy, allowing love and light to flow through us and touch every corner of the world.

Recognizing the interconnectedness of all beings also means acknowledging the interconnectedness of our own being. We are not separate entities but rather multifaceted beings, comprising physical, emotional, mental, and spiritual aspects. By nurturing and harmonizing these different aspects, we attain a state of wholeness and balance, enabling us to radiate our light more brightly.

In the journey towards 5th dimension expansion, let us remember that our individual growth and evolution are intimately connected to the collective awakening. As we expand our consciousness and raise our vibration, we inspire and uplift others, creating a ripple effect that spreads throughout humanity.

Embrace the interconnectedness of all beings. Let it guide your every thought, word, and action. Together, let us weave a vibrant tapestry of love, compassion, and unity, ushering in a new era of light and harmony on Earth.

Understanding Your Soul's Purpose

In the grand tapestry of existence, every soul has a unique purpose. It is the reason behind our journey on this earthly plane, the driving force that propels us forward, and the ultimate fulfilment of our spiritual growth. As light workers, healers, way-showers, and awakening souls, understanding our soul's purpose is crucial to our 5th dimension expansion in 2024 and beyond.

Our soul's purpose goes beyond the mundane tasks and responsibilities that we undertake in our daily lives. It encompasses the deeper meaning and significance of our existence. It is the call from our higher self, urging us to align with our true nature and contribute to the collective consciousness.

Discovering our soul's purpose begins with self-reflection and inner exploration. We must delve deep within ourselves, questioning our desires, passions, and innate talents. What makes our hearts sing? What brings us joy and fulfillment? By seeking answers to these questions, we can uncover the unique gifts and abilities that we possess, which are essential for fulfilling our soul's purpose.

Moreover, our soul's purpose is intricately connected to serving others. As light workers, healers, and way-showers, we feel joy when we participate in the uplifting of humanity's vibration and assisting in the collective awakening. We are here to bring love, healing, and light to those who need it most. By embracing our purpose, we become catalysts for positive change, spreading compassion, wisdom, and inspiration wherever we go.

However, understanding our this part of our soul's purpose is not an instant revelation. It requires patience, introspection, and a willingness to listen to our intuition. We must be open to receiving guidance from the universe, for it is constantly whispering messages and signs to guide us on our path. These signs can come in various forms, such as synchronicities, dreams, or intuitive nudges. By staying present and attuned to these signs, we can navigate our journey with clarity and purpose.

As we embark on our 5th dimension expansion in 2024, it is vital to remember that our soul's purpose evolves and expands alongside our consciousness. It is not a fixed destination but a lifelong journey of growth and transformation. Embrace the process, trust in divine timing, and have faith in your ability to make a profound impact on the world.

In conclusion, understanding your soul's purpose is an integral part of your 5th dimension expansion in 2024. By delving deep within yourself, serving others, and staying attuned to the messages of the universe, you can uncover your unique gifts and contribute to the collective awakening of humanity. Embrace your purpose, for it is the key to unlocking the light within and creating a more harmonious and loving world.

Sharing Your Gifts and Talents

As light workers, healers, way-showers, and awakening souls, you are on a profound journey of self-discovery and expansion. The years 2024-2026 hold great significance for us, as it marks a pivotal moment in our path towards embracing the fifth dimension. Sharing our unique gifts and talents as we navigate this transformative journey is important for humanity's evolution. We have chosen to incarnate now on the planet for this purpose.

Each one of us possesses a set of extraordinary gifts and talents that have been honed over lifetimes. These gifts are not meant to be kept hidden or used solely for personal gain. They are meant to be shared with the world, for the highest good of all. By sharing your gifts, you contribute to the collective awakening and evolution of humanity.

In the fifth dimension, there is a deep understanding that we are all interconnected, and your gifts have a ripple effect that extends far beyond your immediate surroundings. As you step into your true power and express your talents, you inspire others to do the same. Your unique abilities have the potential to ignite a spark within others, helping them remember their own innate gifts and talents.

Sharing your gifts also brings immense joy and fulfillment to your own life. It is through the act of giving that you receive the most profound blessings. When you align with your purpose and share your talents, you tap into a wellspring of abundance and flow. The universe conspires to support you, bringing forth opportunities and connections that further enhance your journey.

However, it is important to remember that sharing your gifts does not mean you have to sacrifice your own well-being. Boundaries and self-care are essential as you navigate this path. Take the time to nurture yourself and replenish your energy so that you can continue to shine your light brightly. When connecting and sharing your energy with others, be mindful of your space and your aura/energy. Cleanse your space after interactions that you find energetically and emotionally draining.

You can do this by imagining a light flowing down over you and through to clear away any lower vibrations. You can sage your aura and workspace, and after each client if working as a healer. Space clearing sprays and oils can be used, always stating your intentions about what you are doing and what you intend to replace the negative energies with.

As you embark on your 5th dimension expansion in 2024, embrace the power of sharing your gifts and talents. Allow your light to shine brightly, illuminating the path for others to follow. Trust in the divine timing and know that the world is ready and waiting for what you have to offer. Together, we can create a world filled with love, compassion, and limitless possibilities.

Serving Others with Compassion

In the journey towards expanding into the 5th dimension, one of the most profound and transformative aspects is the act of serving others with compassion. Our purpose is not only to awaken ourselves but also to uplift and guide others along their own path of awakening.

Compassion is the powerful force that connects us all, transcending boundaries and limitations. It is the pure essence of love, allowing us to see the divine spark within every being we encounter. When we serve others with compassion, we acknowledge and honour the inherent worth and dignity of each individual, recognizing that we are all interconnected and interdependent.

Serving others does not mean sacrificing our own well-being or depleting our energy reserves. It is about finding balance and understanding that we can only give from a place of abundance. By taking care of our own needs first, we can then extend our compassion to others authentically and sustainably.

There are various ways in which we can serve others with compassion including active listening, holding space for others' experiences, and offering support without judgment. We will learn how to cultivate empathy, understanding, and kindness towards ourselves and others, fostering a nurturing environment for growth and healing.

As a healer and light worker, we are the conduit for the light frequencies that we share with other souls. When we offer energetic healing services, we are offering this with compassion for each individual. Such practices such as Reiki, sound healing, and energy clearing techniques, can assist in the awakening process and promote holistic well-being.

CARAELLIOTTHEALINGHOUSE.COM

Ultimately, serving others with compassion is not just a one-time act but a way of life. It is a continuous journey of self-discovery, selflessness, and expansion. As we embrace this path, we not only uplift others but also experience profound personal transformation and growth.

As we embark on our individual journeys towards 5th dimension expansion, let us remember the power of serving others with compassion. Through our actions, we have the ability to create a ripple effect that transcends through time and space and in all dimensions, bringing about a collective awakening and ushering in a new era of love, unity, and harmony.

Together, let us illuminate the world with the light within and create a brighter future for all.

Practicing Compassion and Empathy

In today's fast-paced and often disconnected world, it is more important than ever for light workers, healers, way-showers, and awakening souls to cultivate compassion and empathy. As we embark on our journey towards 5th dimension expansion in 2024, these qualities will serve as the foundation for creating a harmonious and loving world.

Compassion is the ability to recognize and understand the suffering of others and to take action to alleviate it. It is the practice of extending kindness, love, and understanding to all beings, regardless of their background or beliefs. By embodying compassion, we become a beacon of light and hope in a world that often feels dark and chaotic.

Empathy, on the other hand, is the capacity to feel and experience the emotions of others. It is the ability to put ourselves in someone else's shoes and truly understand their perspective. When we cultivate empathy, we are able to connect on a deeper level with those around us, fostering meaningful relationships and promoting healing and transformation.

To practice compassion and empathy, we must first cultivate these qualities within ourselves. This starts with self-compassion, the practice of treating ourselves with kindness and understanding. By acknowledging our own struggles and embracing our imperfections, we create a solid foundation for extending compassion and empathy to others.

One powerful way to develop compassion and empathy is through meditation and mindfulness practices. By quieting our minds and turning inward, we can tap into our innate capacity for love and compassion. Through mindfulness, we learn to be fully present with ourselves and others, allowing us to truly listen and connect with those in need.

Another essential aspect of practicing compassion and empathy is to actively engage in acts of service and kindness. By volunteering our time, donating to causes we believe in, or simply offering a helping hand to those around us, we can make a tangible difference in the lives of others. I encourage you to offer your unique gifts and talents, as you are the only person who can offer what you have as a light worker and healer. By embodying compassion and empathy, we become catalysts for positive change. We have the power to create a world where love, understanding, and unity prevail.

Practicing compassion and empathy is not always easy. It requires patience, self-reflection, and a willingness to step outside of our comfort zones. But the rewards are immeasurable. By awakening the light within ourselves and extending it to others, we contribute to the collective awakening and transformation of humanity.

Let us commit to practicing compassion and empathy in every aspect of our lives. Through time, humanity has lost some of the wisdom of compassionate behavior and therefore we need to practice to be able to embody this. As we do this, we will find peace within ourselves and begin our own contribution to the changes in humanity's frequencies. Together, we can create a world filled with love, understanding, and harmony, one act of kindness at a time.

Being a Beacon of Light and Hope

In the realm of spiritual awakening and consciousness expansion, being a beacon of light and hope is a calling that resonates deeply with light workers, healers, way-showers, and awakening souls. As we embark on our journey to 5th dimension expansion in 2024, it becomes increasingly crucial for us to understand and embrace the power we hold in illuminating the path for others.

Being a beacon of light means embodying the highest vibrational frequencies of love, compassion, and empathy. It requires us to tap into our inner wisdom and connect with the divine essence that resides within us. By doing so, we become a source of inspiration and guidance for those who are seeking a way out of the darkness and into the light.

Hope is the fuel that ignites the flame of transformation. As we navigate the shifting energies of the 5th dimension, it is imperative that we hold onto hope and share it with others. Our collective consciousness has the power to create a ripple effect, spreading positivity and optimism throughout the world. By being a beacon of hope, we help to anchor the energies of love and light, making the journey towards 5th dimension expansion a smoother and more fulfilling experience.

To truly embody the role of a beacon of light and hope, we must first embark on our own personal journey of self-discovery and healing. This involves delving deep into our shadows and embracing the parts of ourselves that we may have previously rejected or ignored. By doing so, we create space for the light to enter and transmute any darkness that may be holding us back.

As we heal and expand our own consciousness, we become a magnet for others who are on a similar path. They are drawn to our energy and seek solace in our presence. It is through our own transformation and growth that we inspire and empower others to embark on their own journey of awakening.

Being a beacon of light and hope is a sacred responsibility that comes with the territory of 5th dimension expansion. As light workers, healers, way-showers, and awakening souls, we have the power to create a profound impact on the world around us. By embodying love, compassion, and empathy, and by holding onto hope, we become catalysts for positive change. Let us embrace this calling with open hearts and minds, knowing that together, we can illuminate the path towards a brighter future.

Cara Elliott Whangamata Beach, New Zealand

Chapter 6: Integration and Expansion

Embracing the Integration Process

As light workers, healers, way-showers, and awakening souls, we find ourselves at the forefront of a profound transformation in consciousness. The journey of expansion into our 5th dimensional vibration, holds immense potential for personal and collective growth. But what does it mean to embrace the integration process? How can we navigate this path with grace and clarity?

Embracing the integration process begins with a deep understanding of what the 5th dimension represents. It is a realm of higher frequencies, where love, unity, and interconnectedness prevail. It is a state of being where we transcend the limitations of the ego and align ourselves with the universal flow of energy. In this dimension, we tap into our innate wisdom and power, co-creating a reality that is aligned with our soul's purpose.

To embark on this journey, we must first cultivate a strong foundation of self-awareness. We need to dive deep within ourselves, exploring the depths of our being and shedding the layers of conditioning that no longer serve us. This inner work is essential for healing old wounds, releasing limiting beliefs, and aligning our thoughts, emotions, and actions with our highest truth.

As we progress on this path, we must also embrace the integration of mind, body, and spirit. This involves nurturing our physical bodies with healthy practices such as mindful movement, nourishing food, and restorative sleep. It also entails cultivating a regular spiritual practice that connects us with our inner guidance, whether through meditation, prayer, or any other form of sacred ritual.

In the process of integration, we must also be open to receiving support and guidance from our spiritual community. Surrounding ourselves with like-minded individuals who share our vision and values can provide invaluable encouragement and inspiration.

Together, we can create a supportive network that uplifts and empowers each other on our respective journeys.

Moreover, embracing the integration process requires allowing the divine timing of our expansion. It is crucial to trust in the wisdom of the universe and to give ourselves permission to flow with the cosmic currents.

Letting go of control and embracing the unknown allows us to connect to the higher intelligence that navigates us towards our highest potential. To let go of control in areas of your life, you need to trust in your ability to manage whatever comes your way, to trust your resilience. As mentioned in earlier chapters, using the transformative process of 'tapping' to change your programed beliefs that keep you fear based. Also regularly clearing and balancing your chakras and aura, through meditation, energy healing, affirmations, soul/ life coaching.

Embodying Higher Frequencies

As light workers, healers, way-showers, and awakening souls, we are all on a remarkable journey towards 5th dimension expansion in 2024. This section, "Embodying Higher Frequencies," is dedicated to guiding you through the process of aligning with and embodying the elevated energies and vibrations of the 5th dimension.

The 5th dimension is a realm of higher consciousness, love, unity, and harmony. It is a space where we transcend the limitations of the 3rd-dimensional reality and tap into our true divine essence. Embodying the higher frequencies of the 5th dimension is not only about reaching a higher state of being but also about becoming a channel for these energies to flow through us and positively impact the world around us.

To begin embodying higher frequencies, it is essential to cultivate a deep sense of self-awareness and self-love. Take the time to connect with your inner self through meditation, breathwork, or any practice that resonates with you. I invite you to connect with a soul coach, to explore soul hypnotherapy, to seek understanding by connecting with your guides and angels.

By quieting the mind and tuning into your inner guidance, you can attune yourself to the frequencies of the 5th dimension. Attending healing sessions, workshops and retreats that give you the opportunity to connect and understand your inner self – your soul self.

Another crucial aspect of embodying higher frequencies is healing and releasing any lower vibrational energies that may be holding you back. This includes addressing past traumas, limiting beliefs, and emotional baggage. Connect with a trusted Life | Soul coach, energy healer who can support you in raising your vibration. By doing the necessary inner work, you can clear the path for the higher frequencies to flow through you effortlessly.

In addition to personal healing, it is also vital to surround yourself with a supportive community of like-minded individuals. Seek out fellow light workers, healers, and awakening souls who are also on the path to 5th dimension expansion. By coming together, you can amplify your collective energy and support one another in embodying the higher frequencies.

Practicing self-care and nurturing your physical, emotional, and spiritual well-being is another key aspect of embodying higher frequencies. Incorporate activities such as yoga, energy healing, sound therapy, or any other practice that resonates with you. These activities not only raise your personal vibration but also assist in integrating the higher frequencies into your physical body.

Remember, embodying higher frequencies is a continuous process. It requires dedication, commitment, and a willingness to let go of old patterns and embrace the new. As you continue on your journey towards 5th dimension expansion in 2024, trust in your own inner light and know that you are an essential part of the collective awakening.

You can align with and embody these elevated energies and vibrations of the 5th dimension. The higher frequencies are already coming into the planet, so embrace this transformative journey and let your light shine brightly as you contribute to the collective shift towards a higher state of consciousness.

Manifesting Abundance in All Areas of Life

We are at the forefront of a profound shift in consciousness. Your journey towards the 5th dimension expansion in 2024 - 2026 is not just about personal growth; it is about transforming the world around you. One of the key aspects of this transformation is manifesting abundance in all areas of life.

Abundance is not limited to just material wealth; it encompasses every aspect of our existence. It is about experiencing joy, love, health, success, and fulfilment in all areas of life. In the 5th dimension, abundance is not something that is earned or deserved; it is our birthright as divine beings. It just is, because the frequency holds the vibration of abundance for all.

To manifest abundance, it is essential to align your thoughts, emotions, beliefs, and actions with the frequency of abundance. This means letting go of scarcity mentality and embracing a mindset of abundance. Start by acknowledging and appreciating the abundance that already exists in your life. Gratitude is a powerful tool that opens the floodgates for more abundance to flow into your life.

Another important element of manifesting abundance is releasing any limiting beliefs or patterns that may be blocking your path. These could be deep-seated beliefs about unworthiness, lack, or fear of success. The power of manifestation comes from within and understanding your journey of self-development and how you have created your own reality throughout your life.

The true reward is self-discovery. When you aim to manifest abundance in all areas of our life, there is a journey to be taken to understand yourself and how you interact with the world around you. When you do this process, you are not only amplifying your ability to create the life you want, you are also deeply healing. Through self-reflection, meditation, and energy healing techniques, you can identify and release blocks, allowing abundance to flow freely.

Visualisation and intention setting are powerful tools for manifesting abundance. Create a clear vision of what abundance means to you in all areas of life – relationships, career, health, and spirituality. See yourself already living in that state of abundance, feeling the emotions of joy, love, and fulfilment. Set clear intentions to manifest this abundant reality and take inspired action towards your goals.

All manifesting requires some understanding of the universal Law of Attraction. This universal law involves the science of quantum physics, psychology and spirituality. The power of positive thinking also contributes to the law of attraction.

Practices like meditation visualisation and journaling, vision boards, lists that are used to cultivate a positive mind-set have, foster self-purpose, improve physical health, and interpersonal relationships.

- Write a list – write what makes your heart sing, put it into action and check it off when completed.
- Share with those around you that love and support you what you want to manifest. The more energy available to create the more the law of attraction becomes amplified.
- Create a Vision Board to remind each day why you are getting out of bed and begin your day

Remember that abundance is not just about receiving; it is also about giving. When you share your gifts, talents, and resources with others, you create a flow of abundance that benefits everyone involved. By serving others, you open yourself up to receiving even more abundance in return.

In your journey of raising your vibration, embrace the power of manifesting abundance in all areas of life. Know that you have the ability to create a reality that is rich in joy, love, success, and fulfilment. By aligning your thoughts, emotions, beliefs, and actions with the frequency of abundance, you can manifest a life beyond your wildest dreams. Step into your power as a divine being and let the abundance flow.

Trusting the Divine Timing of Your Soul's Journey

As we each embark on our unique soul journey, towards self-discovery and spiritual awakening, we are on the forefront of this transformative journey, eagerly seeking to expand our consciousness and align with the higher frequencies of the 5th dimension In this book, "Awakening the Light Within: Your 5th Dimensional Guide," we delve into one of the most profound aspects of this journey - trusting the divine timing of our soul's evolution.

As we navigate through life's trials and triumphs, it is natural to question the timing of our experiences. We wonder why certain situations unfold when they do, or why our dreams seem to elude us. However, in the realm of spiritual growth and ascension, we must learn to surrender to the divine timing orchestrated by the higher forces at play.

Trusting the divine timing of our soul's journey requires faith and patience. It requires us to release the need for control and surrender to the cosmic dance of the Universe. When we try to force outcomes or resist the natural flow, we create resistance and disharmony within ourselves. But when we surrender to divine timing, we open ourselves up to the infinite wisdom and guidance of the Universe.

As mentioned earlier in this book, spiritual practices can help us cultivate trust in the divine timing of our soul's journey. Understanding and practicing meditation, visualization, and affirmations as resources to align ourselves with the higher frequencies and vibrations of the 5th dimension. We also discussed the importance of self-reflection, gratitude, and letting go of thought patterns and behaviors that keep us in the 3rd dimensional vibration. These practices foster a deep sense of trust in the unfolding of our soul's evolution and connect us to our intuition – our soul speak.

CARAELLIOTTHEALINGHOUSE.COM

As we embark on the path to our 5th dimension vibration, let us trust in the divine timing of our soul's journey, knowing that every experience, challenge, and triumph is perfectly orchestrated for our growth and awakening. Together, we can create a world steeped in love, light, and harmony, one soul at a time until collectively we raise our vibrations.

THE PROPHECY OF THE Q'EROS, THE WISE NATIVE OF THE ANDES

"When enough Seeds are awakened, liberated from fear and other negative aspects of the third and fourth level of consciousness, the fifth level seeds can sprout within humanity and form a Whole."

The prophecy announces that, when the fifth level of consciousness is reached, this will be done collectively and simultaneously and that Love and Compassion will be the guiding forces. The Golden Age will announce the beginning of the Sixth Sun, that will be the time for the "Children of Light" who will be fully awake.

Chapter 7: Embracing the 5th Dimension

Navigating the Shift in Consciousness

As light workers, healers, way-showers, and awakening souls, we have been called to be the pioneers of a profound shift in consciousness that is set to occur between 2024 - 2026. This shift marks the transition to the 5th dimension, a higher vibrational plane of existence where love, unity, and spiritual expansion prevail. In order to fully embrace this transformation, it is crucial that we prepare ourselves on all levels – physically, mentally, emotionally, and spiritually.

With so many shifts in consciousness and more to happen in 2024, we are aware that the time lag is shortening. In the 3rd dimension especially, there is a time buffer between thought / intention and manifestation. But as we rise and climb the dimensional layers, that buffer zone dissolves. This means what you engage in through thought, action, emotion, will manifest much faster, almost instantaneously. Many of you will have noticed this.

Many people are awakening and are raising their vibrations. There are also many where this awakening is happening unconsciously. There are a lots of intense feelings / shadow energy rising to be healed and to be transmuted. Navigating other people's feelings, thoughts and actions is important so that you are not reactive and step back into these lower frequency patterns.

As you move through your daily life there will be people who express the lower frequency and will project onto you their pain through blame and judgement. It can be is difficult for all of us to step into full responsibility for our thoughts, feelings and actions. The best thing we can do is to be mindful of this and maintain your own equilibrium. We honor those that are struggling and respect them on their journey.

As light workers and healer and awakening souls, we stay centred. It's easy to engage in a mind-to-mind conversation, where you respond from a reactive standpoint, using ego, mind. Allow others to project and allow them to express their own wounds. You can be kind and considerate and point it out to them their shadow energy with love and kindness. Or say nothing and stay centred. Sometimes non-interference is often the highest form of mastery. Observe, step back and allow it to bounce off your energy field. Do not absorb and take onboard and let it change you.

Remember your purpose for incarnating on the planet at this time is to be a part of the rebirth humanity into these higher frequencies, so we can all care for each other and share the planets resources amongst us all.

The earth will always find balance and restore itself, and we can work with the harmony of the earth to achieve our own balance. We can embrace the divine flow of the planet to alchemize dark and light. We have so much potential in our DNA and as divine beings to raise our vibration and expand our consciousness - ascending into our harmonic 5th dimensional bodies.

One of the first steps in preparing for the shift is to shine a light on the aspects of ourselves, we are unhappy about and want to change and transform these aspects. Such as emotional blockages, negative thought patterns, wanting to control people and events in our lives. When we can begin the process of healing and releasing what no longer serves us, we make way for the higher frequencies of the 5th dimension to flow through us more easily.

Another key aspect of preparation is to prioritize self-care. We must nurture our physical bodies, ensuring they are healthy and vibrant vessels for the divine light that is seeking to flow through us. This can be achieved through regular exercise, a balanced diet, and mindful practices such as yoga or meditation. It doesn't mean we have to 'give up everything', however everything in moderation is a great start to transforming our physical and energy bodies. Taking time for ourselves and engaging in activities that bring us joy and fulfilment is also essential, as it raises our vibration and aligns us with the frequencies of the 5th dimension.

In addition, it is important to surround ourselves with a supportive community of like-minded individuals. Connecting with other light workers, healers, and awakening souls not only provides us with a sense of belonging but also allows for the exchange of knowledge, insights, and experiences. Together, we can support and uplift each other as we navigate this transformative journey.

Lastly, we must remain open and receptive to the guidance and wisdom that comes from within and from higher realms. This can be achieved through practices such as meditation, prayer, and connecting with our spiritual guides and angels. Try using your oracle cards as a way of connecting with your higher self – your soul's voice. By cultivating a deep connection with our inner guidance, we can navigate the shifting energies with grace and ease and allow our intuition to lead the way.

Oracle Cards

Oracle Cards are an inspirational resource to bridge the unseen world of Sprit and the Physical World of our day –to-day lives. They connect us to our intuition, our Soul and tune into spiritual insight with the intention of gaining answers and practical guidance.

A reading consists of a deck of oracle cards, shuffling the deck, selecting the cards, arraigning them in a particular 'spread' or 'layout' and interpreting the messages/meaning of the pictures and words in relation to the question asked.

It is worth spending time to clarify your questions so that you ask a question you really need to know the answer to and that it is clear what you are asking. Start with a simple question - A beginning question such as "What do I need to know today?" "What do I need to look at in my life right now?"

When shuffling the cards, take a breath and be present as you do this, and allow your energy to merge with the energy of the cards.

What to do when you have your chosen oracle card(s)?

- To read each card look at the picture and words and symbols on each card carefully and absorb the message that is being given to you.

- Notice what you first feel and first thoughts are about the message, this is your intuition/inner guide hearing/seeing the message given to you from your spirit guides and angels.

- If you want a deeper experience with the cards, jot it down—in sentences, phrases, single words, or doodles. (May help you digest the messages better).

- Usually your initial intuitive thought/feeling are the most profound. Expect some of these to come as surprises—guidance or insight you had never considered before.

- Sit with the cards calmly for a minute or two and see what floats to the surface.

The Soul Loves the Truth: When you ask the question, you're sending a message to yourself / the Universe / God / Source of all things, that you are seeking to live a happy life and are open to guidance about how to make this happen.

As we prepare for the shift in consciousness and our 5th dimension expansion in 2024 - 2026, let us remember that this is a collective journey. We are all in this together, and our individual growth and expansion contribute to the collective awakening of humanity. Let us embrace this opportunity with open hearts and open minds, knowing that we are here for a purpose and that our light is needed now more than ever. Together, we can create a world filled with love, unity, and infinite possibilities.

Anchoring Light and Love on Earth

In the grand tapestry of the universe, Earth has always been a unique and sacred place. It is a realm where the energies of light and love converge, and where the potential for spiritual growth and transformation is unparalleled. As light workers, healers, way-showers, and awakening souls, we have been called upon to play a pivotal role in anchoring these divine energies on Earth, elevating the collective consciousness, and paving the way for the magnificent expansion of the 5th dimension in 2024.

The journey towards anchoring light and love on Earth begins with our own inner transformation. We must first awaken the light within ourselves, embracing our true essence and aligning with our divine purpose. As we embark on this journey, we become beacons of light, radiating love and compassion to all those around us. Through our thoughts, words, and actions, we have the power to uplift and inspire others, igniting the spark of awakening within them.

To anchor light and love on Earth, it is essential that we cultivate a deep connection with the higher realms. Through meditation, prayer, and spiritual practices, we open ourselves up to receive divine guidance and wisdom. We become channels for the cosmic energies, allowing them to flow through us and into the world. By consciously connecting with the higher dimensions, we bring forth healing and transformation, not only for ourselves but for the entire planet.

As we navigate the path of anchoring light and love, we must also remember the importance of unity and collaboration. We are not alone in this journey, for there are countless other souls who share our mission. By joining forces, we amplify our efforts and create a powerful ripple effect of positive change. Together, we can create a harmonious and loving world, where peace, joy, and abundance abound.

In the years 2024 - 2026, the energies of the 5th dimension will reach their peak, creating a profound shift in consciousness. As light workers, healers, way-showers, and awakening souls, we are at the forefront of this transformation. We are being asked to anchor these divine energies on Earth, birthing a new era of love and enlightenment. Blessed Be.

The time is now. Let us rise together, embracing our roles as catalysts for change. Let us anchor light and love on Earth, creating a beautiful tapestry of unity and harmony. Our journey to 5th dimension expansion in 2024 begins within each of us, as we awaken the light within and radiate love to the world. Together, we can create a future filled with limitless possibilities, where the Earth shines brightly as a beacon of light in the universe.

Radiating Positivity and Peace

Humanity is undergoing a 'shift' and 'upgrade' into a higher dimension of spiritual consciousness. In this journey towards our 5th dimensional consciousness, radiating positivity and peace becomes an essential aspect of our transformation. As light workers, healers, way-showers, and awakening souls, we hold a profound responsibility to not only raise our own vibrations but also to inspire and uplift others on their path.

At the core of radiating positivity is the understanding that our thoughts and emotions have a direct impact on our reality. As we align with higher frequencies, we become aware of the power we possess to create our own experiences. By consciously choosing positive thoughts and emotions, we can shift our energetic vibration, attracting more harmonious circumstances into our lives. This not only benefits us individually but also contributes to the collective consciousness, assisting in the overall ascension process.

Embracing peace is another crucial element on this journey. Peace is not merely the absence of conflict; it is a state of being that emanates from within. By cultivating inner peace through practices such as meditation, breathwork, and mindfulness, we become a beacon of tranquility in a world often overshadowed by chaos. In this state of calm, we have the ability to transmit peace to others, triggering a ripple effect that can positively influence the collective.

One powerful technique to radiate positivity and peace is through the practice of heart coherence. By intentionally shifting our focus to your heart center (chakra) and cultivating feelings of love, gratitude, and compassion, we activate the electromagnetic field of the heart. This coherent heart field not only enhances our personal well-being but also has a profound impact on those around us. As light workers and healers, tapping into heart coherence enables us to touch the lives of others, helping them navigate their own awakening journey.

The awareness of healing and embodiment of this higher frequency is 'what you do', to connect with your own alignment of truth and peace. Take responsibility for moving from, following what others say and do, to what is in alignment in your heart. Humanity has been through many cycles of dysfunctional expressions of itself leaving us with cultural and societal influences that we assume our true but are not necessarily in alignment with your own truth.

These cycles continue to manifest through time, and it can be difficult to re-create ourselves within these experiences. We have to step out of this conditioning and create a new identity, a new vibration through various spiritual practices that have been discussed in this book. Only then can we deepen the awareness of our own ever-expanding consciousness.

One way to embrace these higher vibrations is by radiating positivity and peace in our words and our actions. This does not mean denying or suppressing negative emotions. Instead, it involves acknowledging and transforming them through conscious awareness and self-compassion. By integrating all aspects of ourselves, we can transmute lower vibrations into higher frequencies, contributing to our own expansion and the collective transformation.

As we embark on our journey towards 5th dimensional expansion in 2024, embodying positivity and peace becomes a powerful catalyst for growth and healing. By radiating these qualities, we not only uplift ourselves but also become catalysts for the transformation of others. Together, as a collective of light workers, healers, way-showers, and awakening souls, we can create a world infused with love, harmony, and peace.

Co-creating a New Earth in the 5th Dimension

As the New Earth is evolving, and we are entering 2024, the energies on our planet are shifting, and a new era of consciousness is arising. As light workers, healers, way-showers, and awakening souls are you ready to embark on a transformative journey towards your 5th dimensional body?

The 5th dimension represents a higher level of consciousness, where love, unity, and oneness prevail. It is a dimension of heightened awareness, where individuals are deeply connected to their divine essence and the collective consciousness. In this realm, the limitations of the 3rd dimension, such as fear, separation, and ego-driven desires, are transcended, allowing for a more harmonious and fulfilling experience of life.

In order to co-create a New Earth in the 5th dimension, it is crucial for each individual to embark on their personal journey of awakening. Your unique gifts and abilities are needed to guide and support others on their path towards 5th dimension expansion. By embracing your true essence and stepping into your power, you become beacons of light, inspiring others to awaken and remember their divine nature.

Co-creation is a key aspect of manifesting a New Earth in the 5th dimension. It requires collaboration, unity, and a shared vision. As you connect with like-minded souls, you will find strength in numbers and create a powerful collective energy that can bring about profound change.

Together, you can envision and manifest a world where love, compassion, and harmony reign supreme. Together as 'new humans' we can anchor in the light moving through the planet and create the framework for the new Golden Earth. This will allow us to access the higher streams of consciousness (advanced universal intelligence) enabling us to make heart felt connections with humanity and other civilizations.

As we are already witnessing the emergence of incredible new technologies, innovations and galactic contact, this Age of Aquarius will bring forth the higher frequencies and energies that will allow us to communicate in ways we have not imagined yet. Raising our vibrations and expanding our consciousness allows us access to these exiting possibilities as we move through humanities ascension.

By awakening the light within, you are not only transforming your own life but also contributing to the collective awakening and the birth of a New Earth. Embrace this incredible opportunity, for you are here for a reason, and the world needs your light more than ever.

I invite you to be a conscious co-creator of the New Earth, raising your vibration to the highest frequency available to us on the planet now - the 5th Dimension of Love and Light.

Travelling the road of life, the soul's journey at this present time on Earth, is to find the balance between being a spiritual being having a human experience.

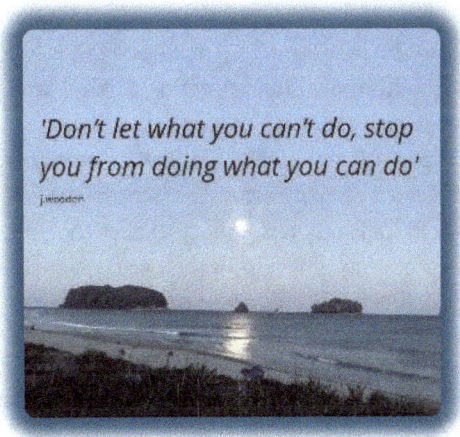

Whangamata, New Zealand

The Key for Change

With this knowledge, please realise, comes the responsibility of sharing it.

"Throughout the Universe there is order, in the movement of plants, in nature in the functioning of the human mind.
A mind that, in its natural state of order, is in harmony with the universe, and is such timeless.
Your life is an expression of your mind. You are the creator of your own Universe.
For as a human being, you are free to will whatever you desire, through the use of your thoughts and your words, there is great power there.
It can be a blessing or a curse, it's entirely up to you.
For the quality of your life is brought about by the quality of your thinking, think about that!
Thoughts produce actions, look at what you are thinking. See the pettiness & the envy & the greed & the fear & all the other attitudes that cause you discomfort.
Realise that the one thing that you have absolute control over is your attitude.
See the effect it has on those around you, for each life is linked to all life.
And your words carry with them chain reactions, like a stone that is thrown into a pond.
If you're thinking is in order, your words will flow directly from the heart, creating ripples of love. If you truly want to change your world my friends, you must change your thinking. Reason is your greatest tool, it creates an atmosphere of understanding which leads to caring, which is love. Choose your words with care, go forward with love".

Author unknown

References & Resources

Cara Elliott HealingHouse www.caraelliotthealinghouse.com
Foundation & Advanced Crystal Healing Course (online)
www.caraelliotthealinghouse.com/onlinecourses
Channeled information from my spirit guides. Cara Elliott
Channelings from Jimmy for Cara. via Clint Bluesky. @blusky_74
Brennan, Barbara Ann. (1993) "Light Emerging- The journey of personal healing". USA
Chan, Anna. Soul Hypnotherapy. www.beyondtheveil.co.nz/hypnotherapy/
PSYCH-K® www.psych-k.com/
ThetaHealing™ www.thetahealinginstituteofknowledge.com/
Satori, Judy. (2011) "Sunshine before the dawn"
Silverman, Debra. www.debrasilvermanastrology.com/
Tipping, Colin. www.radicalforgiveness.org/

www.ingramcontent.com/pod-product-compliance
Lightning Source LLC
Chambersburg PA
CBHW071838290426
44109CB00017B/1856